REFLECTIONS ON POLITICAL IDEOLOGIES

REFLECTIONS ON POLITICAL IDEOLOGIES

DR. P. B. RATHOD
M.A., Ph.D.
Reader
Deptt. of Political Science,
Gulbarga University,
GULBARGA

Commonwealth

Reflections on Political Ideologies

1st Edition : 2006
ISBN 81-311-0057-X

Published by :
Commonwealth Publishers
4831/24, Prahlad Street,
Ansari Road, Darya Ganj,
New Delhi - 110002
Phone : 23272541, 23257835
Fax : 91-011-23257835
e-mail : Campusbooks@hotmail.com

Laser Typesetting by :
Stylish Laser Typesetter
Delhi

Printed at :
Roshan Offset Printers
Delhi

FOREWORD

Dr. P.B. Rathod is a men of ideas and also a prolific writer. His writings indicates his multifaceted personality. I have great pleasure in writing to Dr. P.B. Rathod book on "Reflections on Political Ideologies". It is a book worth reading not only by the students and professors of political science course, but also the candidates appearing for I.A.S., I.P.S., I.F.S. and other allied services.

The book is divided into eight chapters. The first chapter highlights the Meaning and Implications of Political Ideologies. In the second chapter, the learned writer narrated about conservatism. In the third chapter, the author illustrated about Socialism and Its Contributors. In the fourth chapter, Dr. Rathod narrated about Democratic Socialism. In the fifth chapter, the aforesaid author described about Environmentalism. In the sixth chapter, the writer fully devoted his attention to Feminism and its various movements. In the seventh chapter, Dr. Rathod exhaustively discussed about Anarchism. In the eighth chapter, Dr. Rathod has not forgotten to write about liberalism and Fascism. In the last chapter, the learned writer explained about Fascism and Nazism.

The speciality of the book is that at the end Dr. Rathod has given glossary of political thinkers, glossary of terms and concepts and select bibliography. Lastly, I wish the author all the success in his academic career.

Dr. B.R. Patil
Director
Distance Education
Gulbarga University, Gulbarga

ACKNOWLEDGEMENT

I am fully and deeply indebted to my parents and elder brothers to complete this burden some and heavy work. My sincere thanks are due to Prof. V.B. Coutinho, Vice-Chancellor, Gulbarga University, Gulbarga for his constant encouragement in academic work. My thanks are due to my wife (Mrs.) Vimala, daughters Kaveri, Priyanka, Premalata and Sons Rajesh and Harish who always extended moral support and encouragement to me in completing this book.

Lastly, I thank Ajay Verma, Commonwealth Publishers, New Delhi for timely publishing this book.

Dr. P. B. Rathod

CONTENTS

1

MEANING AND NATURE OF POLITICAL IDEOLOGIES

(A) INTRODUCTION

The word ideology coming from the Greek bios, or is the scientific study of life.[1] Psychology is the study of psyche, or mind. And "Sociology" is the study of society. It seems only logical, then, that ideology would be the scientific study of ideas. And that is just what "ideology" originally meant when the term was coined in the eighteenth century in France. Over the last two centuries, however, the meaning of the term has shifted considerably. Rathor than the scientific study of ideas, "ideology" has come to refer to a set of ideas that tries to link thought with action. That is, ideologies attempt to shape how people think and therefore how they act.[2] Ideology is called as a political doctrine or formula. Ideology is first of all concerned with values. That is how we ought to treat each other and live together in society. Thus, it embodies the values. Political ideologies are dynamic. They do not stand still, they adjust to changing conditions. There is a every shift in political winds. Ideologies try to shape direct social change. Changes are always taking place.

Belief, Action and Tradition

Ideologies, then, are guides to political action. They give us ideals to believe in, tell us for what goals to strive and for what causes to fight. They thereby give the individual believer a sense of identity and a sense of purpose. One can see one self as a liberal working for human rights, a nationalist working for one's country's freedom, a revolutionary socialist working to overthrow the capitalist system, or a women challenging the power of patriarchy, all on behalf of some part of humanity, yet thereby working for the ultimate good of humanity as such.[3]

Ideologies can tell us what policies to pursue, who are our friends and enemies, and why rival beliefs are at best wrong and dangerous. Ideologies can, therefore, inspire common action and satisfy our aspiration or to create or preserve the best possible world in which all, or at least these most worthy, socialism fulfilment. To make sense of our present ideological preoccupation we need to look back. Ideological thinking is at least as old as the Ancient Greeks.[4]

An ideology, more precisely, performs four functions for people who hold it. The 1. Explanatory, 2. Evaluative, 3. Orientative, and 4. Programmatic functions. Let us look more closely at these four functions.

1. Explanation

An ideology offers an explanation of why social, political and economic conditions are as they are, particularly in times of crisis. At such times people will search for some explanation of what is happening. Why are there wars? Why do depressions occur? What causes unemployment? Why some people rich and others poor? To these and many other questions, different ideologies supply different answers.[5] But in one way or another, every ideology tries to answer these questions and to make sense of the complicated world in which we live.

2. Evaluation

The second function of ideologies is to supply standards for evaluating social conditions. There is a difference, after all, between explaining why certain things are happening and deciding whether those things are good or bad. Are all wars evils to be avoided, or are some morally justifiable? Are depressions a normal part of the business cycle or a symptom of a sick economic system? Is full employment a reasonable ideal or a native pipe dream? Are vast disparities of wealth between rich and poor desirable or undesirable? Are racial tensions inevitable or avoidable? Again, an ideology supplies its followers with the criteria required for answering these and other questions. If you are a libertarian, for example, you are likely to evaluate a proposed policy by asking if it increases or decreases the role of government in the lives of the individuals. If it increases government's role, it is undesirable. If you are a feminist, you will probably ask whether this proposed policy will work for or against the interests of women, then either approve or disapprove of it on that basis or if you are a communist, you are apt to ask how this proposal affects the working class and whether it raises or lowers the prospects of their victory in the class struggle. This means that those who follow one ideology may evaluate favourably something that the followers of a different ideology greatly dislike—communists look upon class struggle as a good thing, for instance, while fascists regard it as an evil.[6] Whatever the position may be, however, it is clear that all ideologies provide standards or cues that help people assess, Judge, and appraise social policies and conditions so that they can decide whether those policies and conditions are good, bad or indifferent.

3. Orientation

An ideology supplies its holder with an orientation and a sense of identity of who he or she is, the group (race, nation, sex, and so on) to which he or she belongs, and how he or she is related to the rest of the world. Just as hikers and travellers use maps, compasses, and landmarks to find their way in unfamiliar territory, so people need something to find their social identity and location. Like a compass, ideologies help people orient themselves to gain a sense of where they are, who they are, and how they fit into a complicated world.[7] If you are a communist, for example, you most likely think of yourself as a member of the working class who belongs to a party devoted to freeing workers from capitalist exploitation and oppression, and therefore, implacably opposed to the ruling capitalist class. Or if you are a Nazi you probably think of yourself as a white person and member of a party dedicated to preserving racial purity and enslaving or even eliminating "inferior" races.[8] Or if you are a feminist, you are apt to think of yourself as first and foremost a women (or a men sympathetic or women's problems) who belongs to a movement aiming to end sexual oppression and exploitation. Other ideologies enable their adherents to orient themselves, to see their situation or position in society, in still other ways, but all perform the function of orientation.

4. Political Programme

An ideology finally, tells its followers what to do and how to do it. It performs a programmatic or prescriptive function by setting out a general programme of social and political action. Just as doctors prescribe medicine for their patients and trainers provide a programme of exercise for their clients, so political ideologies prescribe remedies for sick societies and treatments designed to keep the healthy in good health. If an ideology provides a diagnosis of social conditions that leads you to believe that conditions are bad and growing worse, it will not be likely to win your support unless it can also supply a prescription or programme for action that seems likely to improve matters.[9] And this is exactly what ideologies try to do. If you are a communist, for example, you believe it important to raise working class consciousness or awareness in order to prepare for the overthrow of capitalism, the seizure of state power, and the eventual creation of co-operative, communist society. If you are a Nazi, however, you think it important for the "superior" white race to isolate, separate, subordinate and perhaps exterminate—jews, blacks, and other "inferior" peoples. If you are a libertarian, your political programme will include proposals for reducing or eliminating government interference in people's lives. But if you are a traditional conservative, you may want the state or government to intervene in order to promote morality or traditional values. Different ideologies will recommend very different programme of action, as these examples demonstrate, but all will recommend a programme of some sort.[10]

Political ideologies perform these four functions because they are trying to link thought—ideas and beliefs—to action. Every ideology provides a vision of the social and political world as it is, and as it should be in hopes of inspiring people to act either to change or preserve their way of life. If it does not do this—if it does not perform all four functions—it is not a political ideology. In this way our functional definition helps to sharpen our picture of what an ideology is by showing us what it is–and is not.[11]

One thing, an ideology is not a scientific theory. To be sure, the distinction between an ideology and a scientific theory is sometimes difficult to draw. One reason for this is that the proponents of political ideologies often claim that their views are truly scientific.[12] Another reason is that scientists, particularly Social Scientists, sometimes fail to see that their ideological biases are shaping their theories. And political ideologies frequently borrow from scientific theories to help explain. Why the world is as it is. Some anarchists and some liberals have used Darwin's theory of evolution of evolution for their own purposes for instance, as have Nazi's and some communists. Difficult as it may sometimes be to separate the two, this does not mean that there is no difference between a theory and an ideology.[13]

Scientific Theories are empirical in nature, which means that they are concerned with describing and explaining some feature or features of the world, not with prescribing what people ought to do. To the extent that these theories carry implications for how people can live, of course, they also carry implications for the normative problem of how people should live.[14] This is especially true of theories of society, where empirical and normative concerns are remarkably difficult some say impossible to separate. But to say that scientific theories have implications for action is not to accept that they are ideologies. The scientist is not directly concerned as a scientist with these implications, but the ideologue certainly is.[15]

Further, we can also use our functional definition to distinguish political ideologies from some of the other "isms", such as terrorism, that are occasionally mistaken for ideologies. Some people conclude that all "isms" must be political ideologies. This is clearly a mistake. Whatever else they are, alcoholism, magnetism, and hypnotism are not political ideologies.[16] Nor is terrorism. Terrorism may offer a programme for social and political action, thus performing the programmatic function, but it does not itself explain and evaluate conditions or provide people with an orientation. Terrorism is a strategy that some ideologues use to try to advance their causes, but it is not itself an ideology.

Again, similar problem arise with regard to religion. Most religions, perhaps all, perform the explanatory, evaluative, orientative, and programmatic functions, for their followers. Does this mean they are ideologies? It does if we define an ideology to be simply a "belief system", as some scholars propose. Still, there is an important difference between religions and political ideologies. Religions are often concerned with the supernatural and divine with God (or gods) and after life (or after lives). While ideologies are much more interested in the here and now, with this life on this earth. Rather than prepare people for a better life in the next world, in other words, political ideologies aim to help them live as well as possible in this.[17]

This, again is a matter of degree. Most religions take an active interest in how people live on earth, but this is neither always nor necessarily their main concern. For a political ideology, it is. Even so, drawing sharp and dear distinctions between political ideologies, on the one hand, and scientific theories, political philosophies (political ideologies draw on the works of the great political philosophers, to promote their causes. Political ideologies tend to simplify the ideas of political philosophers in order to make them accessible and inspiring to masses of people. The difference between political philosophy and political ideology, then, is largely a difference of degree) and religions, on the other, is not the most important point for someone who wants to understand ideologies. The most important point is to see how the different ideologies perform the four functions and how they make use of various theories, philosophies and religious beliefs in order to do so.

Freedom

Every ideology claims and extend "freedom" (or its synonym, "liberty").[18] But different ideologies define freedom in different ways. This is because freedom is an essentially contested concept. What counts as being free is a matter of controversy, in other words, because there is no one indisputably correct definition of freedom.

Because every ideology claims to promote "freedom", that concept provides a convenient basis for comparing and contrasting different ideologies. According to MacCallum, every conception of freedom includes three features. But what of political freedom? According to MacCallum, people have different views of what counts as freedom in politics because they identify A, B and C in different ways. Let us examine each of these, beginning with the agent, proceeding to a consideration of the agent's goats, and returning to examine the barriers or obstacles facing the agent in pursuing those goals.

1. The Agent

The agent can be an individual, a class, a groups, a nation, a sex, a race, or even a species. Liberals typically talk of freedom as the freedom of the individual. Marx and the Marxists, by contrast, focus their attention on the freedom of a particular class—the working class. Mussolini and the Italian Fascists identified the agent as a nation state, German fascists (Nazis), as a race. For feminists the gender identity of the agent is all important.

2. The Goal

Agents have goals. Different kinds of agents have different kinds of goals. A Nazi's goal is the "purity" and supremacy of the white race. A communist's goal is the achievement of a classless communist society. A liberal's goal is to live in his or her own way, without under interference from others. A feminist's goal is to live in a society that recognizes and rewards the capacities and worth of women. And so on for all other ideologies.[19]

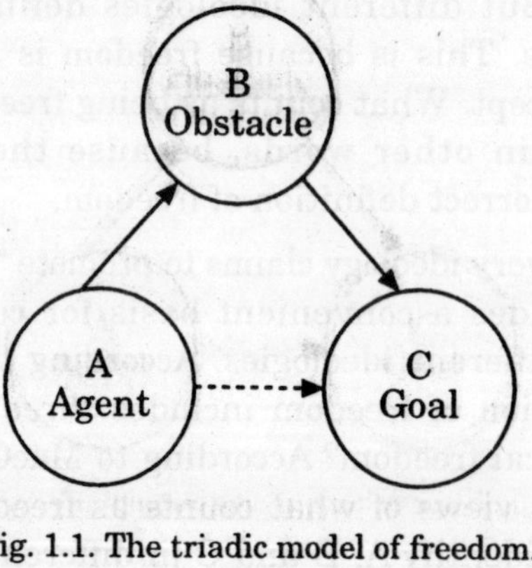

Fig. 1.1. The triadic model of freedom.

3. Obstacles

In pursuing their goals, agents often encounter obstacles in their path. These obstacles can take a variety of forms–material or physical conditions (poverty or physical disabilities, for instance), crime, social, political and economic ideas, ideologies, institutions, practices, traditions and beliefs. Women confront sexism and sexual discrimination. Communists confront the apathy and "false consciousness" of the workers and the wealth and power of the capitalist class. Nazi's confront jews, blacks and other "inferior" races. Ideologies also frequently see other ideologies as obstacle or barriers to be removed. Fascists, for instance, see the liberal emphasis on the individual and the socialist emphasis on equality as obstacles in the way of a united, disciplined, and free society. Whatever form the obstacles take, they must be overcome or removed. The more obstackes these agents can remove, the freer they will be. To the degree that they are unable to overcome the barriers, they are not free, but "unfree". And when the individuals or class or race or gender a political ideology takes to be its agent are not free to realise their goals—then the ideology will call for action to remove the obstacles to their freedom. Throughout the history of political ideologies, that action has often taken the form of revolution.[20]

Ideology and Revolution

Like the revolution of the earth around the sun, a political revolution was a revolving back to a starting point. But after the American and French revolutions of the eighteenth century, "revolution" took on a more radical meaning. The American revolution may have begun as an attempt to restore the colonists rights as Englishmen, but it ended with the creation of a new country with a new system of government. Then, while that new system was still taking shape, the French Revolution began with the intention not of returning to the old ways, but of introducing a radically new social and political order. It bring about sweeping changes in the social, economic, and political life of France. Indeed, the French Revolution sent shock waves through all of Europe and much of the rest of the world waves so strong that their effects are still fell today.[21]

Modern revolutionaries do not simply want to replace one set of rulers or leaders with another nor to make minor changes or reforms in the political structure. Their aim is to overthrow the old order, which they believe to be fundamentally rotten or corrupt. Changes or reforms are not enough in their view, if the government and society are diseased at the roots. When this is the case, they say, the only solution is to uproot the whole social order and replace it with something better. This is literally a radical approach, for the word "radical" comes from the Latin radix, meaning root.

Of course, people will not undertake anything so radical as a revolution unless they believe that it is indeed possible to bring about a fundamental change for the better in society. This is why, conservatives tend to be suspicious of revolutions, their low estimate of human nature generally leads then to believe that sweeping improvements in society are practically impossible. Conservatism is very different from the other ideologies in this respect, however. All of the others hold that human reason and action can bring about great advances in society, politics, and the quality of life. Each ideology has its own idea of what counts as an advance or improvement, to be sure, but all except conservatism have been generally optimistic about the possibility of dramatic progress and significant improvement in the quality of human life.[22]

In this respect, political ideologies are products of the modern world. In earlier times, most people had every reason to believe that their lives would be much the same as their parents and grandparent's lives. Most people made their living from the soil or the sea, and changes in their ways of life were so slow in coming that they usually had little reason to believe that their children's or grandchildren's lives would be significantly different from their own. In the modern world, however, the pace of change has become so rapid that we now have futurists (or futurologists) who make careers of anticipating the changes to come; others, meanwhile, fear that they will not be able to adjust or keep up with change as their jobs and perhaps even their attitudes become obsolete. For better or worse, we live in an age of innovation. And ours, for better or worse, is also an age of ideology. Now-a-days human life and society can and should be dramatically changed. It is this conviction that inspires people to lead or join movements to reshape and even revolutionize their societies. It is this conviction, in short, that gives rise to political ideologies.

Nationalism and Anarchism

Two important political forces remain to be discussed in this introductory chapter. These forces, nationalism and anarchism are often considered ideologies in their own right. Nationalism and anarchism take so many forms and are so entwined with so many different ideologies that we think it better not to treat them as distinct ideologies. Few nationalists are simply nationalists, for instance. They are, instead, liberal or conservative or communist or fascist nationalists. Anarchists are also divided, with most of them following either liberalism or socialism to their extreme conclusions.

Contrary to popular misconception, anarchy does not mean chaos or confusion, nor do anarchists favour chaos and confusion. The word comes from the Greek an archos, meaning "no rule" or "no government". It means abolishing the state, replacing its coercive force with voluntary co-operation among freely consenting and cooperating individuals. As the anarchist sees it, government by its very nature is immoral and evil. All governments force people to do things, they do not want to do—pay taxes, fight in wars, follow orders, and so on—so all governments engage in immoral coercive actions. Anarchist believes that the state is not necessary, but simply evil. Given the chance, anarchists insist, people can live together peacefully and prosperously with no coercive authority over them.

All anarchists agree, then, that the state is an evil to be abolished in favour of a system of voluntary co-operation. But there the agreement ends. Some anarchists are radical individualists who advocate a competitive, capitalist—but stateless society. Some anarchists advocate the violent overthrow of the state, others are pacifists who believe that only a peaceful path can lead to a co-operative society. As one student of anarchism has said, "anarchism is not really an ideology, but rather the point of intersection of several ideologies."

Like nationalism, anarchism has played a major part in the development of modern political ideologies. In the late nineteenth and early twentieth centuries, in particular, it was a significant political force in many parts of the world. Since then, however, its influence has waned. Small band of anarchists continue to argue that the state is immoral and that anarchy is possible but few now take direct action against the state.[23]

Conclusion

We began by noting how important ideologies are in the conflicts that characterize modern political life. We then defined "ideology" as a more or less coherent and comprehensive set of ideas that performs four functions for those who accept it : 1. It explains why social conditions are the way they are; 2. It evaluate those conditions; 3. It orients people so that can see how they fit into society; and 4. It prescribes programme for social and political action. In every ideology, moreover, there are core assumptions about human nature and freedom-assumptions that have led most of them, at one time or another, to call for revolution. In later chapters we will examine the history and structure of different ideologies.[24]

REFERENCES

1. For accounts of the origin and history of "Ideology" see Terrell Carver, "Ideology" in Terence Ball and Richard Daggar, eds., Ideas and Ideologies. A Reader, 3rd ed., 1989, pp. 266-291.
2. Terence Ball and Richard Daggar, Political Ideologies and the Democratic Ideal, New York, 1998, pp. 1-18.

3. *Ibid., op. cit.,* pp. 25-30.
4. Lichtheim, George, The Concept of Ideology, and other Essays, New York : Random House, 1967.
5. Miller, David, Anarchism, London : Dent, 1984.
6. Pfaff, William, The Wrath of Nations : Civilization and the Furies of Nationalism, New York : Simon and Schuster, 1993.
7. Yack Bernard, The Tonging of Total Revolution, Princeton, NJ : Princeton University Press, 1986.
8. Gerald MacCallum, Jr., "Negative and Positive Freedom", Philosophical Review 76 (1967) : 312-334.
9. Berlin Isaiah, Four Essays on Liberty, Oxford : Oxford University Press, 1969.
10. Arendt, Hannah, On Revolution, New York : Viking, 1963.
11. Carter, April, The Political Theory of Anarchism, London : Routledge and Kegan Paul, 1971.
12. Dunn, John, "Revolution", Political Innovation and Conceptual Change, Cambridge : Cambridge University Press, 1989, pp 45-50.
13. Kohn Hans, Nationalism : Its Meaning and History, Princeton, NJ : D. Van Nostrand, 1955.
14. Miller David, Anarchism, London : Dent, 1984.
15. Woodcock, George, Anarchism, Harmondsworth : Penguin, 1963.
16. Wolff, Robert Paul, In Defence of Anarchism.
17. Dunn John, *op. cit., Ibid.,* pp. 52-60.
18. *Ibid., op. cit.,* pp. 65-70.
19. *Ibid., op. cit.,* pp. 72-80.
20. *Ibid., op. cit.,* pp. 82-92.
21. David Miller, *op. cit.,* pp. 85-90.
22. *Ibid., op. cit.,* pp. 93-95.
23. *Ibid., op. cit.,* pp. 96-100.
24. Woodcock, George, *op. cit.,* pp. 102-110.

(B) IMPLICATIONS OF IDEOLOGIES

Ideology is loosely defined as 'belief system'.[1] In this view political ideology is looked at as a set of political beliefs that characterise any group, government or the entire nation.[2] A set of political ideas constitute on ideology.[3] Liberalism, Nationalism, Fascism, Socialism, Communism and the like are all major sets of ideas whose role in the secular politics of a country can very well be understood.[4] Thus, the different sets of ideas are known as 'ideologices'.[5] Thus ideology means the 'Science of ideas'[6]. 'Ideology' is the literal translation of the science of ideas.[7]

Now-a-days, ideology has become a very important concept of political theory.[8] In its broadest sense, the term ideology signifies a set of ideas ranging from one desiring no change in the prevailing order to anther crying for a total transformation of society.[9] Thus, liberalism, conservatism, marxism and nationalisms are all ideologies.[10] Ideologies contain in varying proportions, elements of explanation, justification and faith or belief.[11]

Ideology is action–oriented.[12] The test of a political ideology lies in its applications.[13] Ideology involves commitment and action as a part of the political process.[14] It may or may not possess a logical or philosophical character at all, but it must possess a political character, *i.e.,* a content without which it cannot be described an ideology—a guide to direct political action.[15] Ideology also differs from philosophy.[16] As such, political ideology and political philosophy cannot be regarded as synonymous terms.

Implications

1. Ideology is not the same as values and attitudes of the political culture.[17] It is both a programme for action and an instrument of evaluation.[18]

2. Ideologies do change.[19] An ideology is impossible to translate directly into practice, there has to be accommodation to political realities.[20]

3. Ideologies may be classified according to their role in relation to the political system as rightist or leftist, reactionary or progressive, conservative or revolutionary, reformist or radical and the like.[21] No political system is, however, absolutely free from the bond of ideology.[22]

4. It is the ideology that constitutes the keystone of the arch of a political party or a group.[23] It may be found that a Scuffle between two leaders or between two groups is conducted within the framework of ideological arguments.[24]

5. An ideology being a set of ideas cannot sustain itself if it stems from faith.[25] Since it reflects metaphysical and abstract notions, it should be based on proper scientific analysis, and political action should be directed towards the objective requirements of the society.[26]

6. Ideology has become an instrument whereby the leaders motivate people to take part in political actions, or they accord the character of 'legitimacy' to their political system.[27]

Characteristics of Ideology

1. The goal to which modern ideologies address themselves are typically utopian.[28] They tend to define their goals in unrealistically optimistic terms.[29]

2. Modern ideologies have developed the habit of thinking in over-simplified terms of we versus they, friend versus enemy, freemen versus tyrants, proletarians versus capitalists, patriots versus imperialists.[30] Such clear-cut alternatives are typical of the ideological way of seeing political realities.[31]

3. Modern ideologies draw sustenance from extreme optimism of their views regarding human progress.[32]
4. They deal with the questions : Who will be the rulers? How will the rulers be selected? By what principles will they govern?[33]
5. They constitute an argument, that is, they are intended to persuade to counter opposing views.[34]
6. They integrally affect some of the major values of life.[35]
7. They embrace a programme for the defence of the reform or abolition of important social institutions.[36]
8. They are, in part, nationalisations of group interests—but not necessarily the interests of all groups espousing them.[37]
9. They are normative, ethical, moral in tone and content.[38]
10. They are (inevitably) torn from their context in a broader belief system, and share the structural and stylistic properties of that system.[39]

Besides, most ideologies have these qualities also :

1. They are group beliefs that individuals borrow, most people acquire an ideology by identifying (or disidentifying) with a social group.[40]
2. They have a body of sacred documents (constitutions, bills of rights, manifestos, declarations), heroes (founding fathers, seers and sages, originators and great interpreters).[41]

Functions

1. Evaluate distribution and exercise of political power and the working of political institutions;[42]
2. To rouse people to action and to mobilise political movements;[43]

3. To provide a distinctive language or vocabulary to facilitate the process of examination of political regimes;[44] and
4. To provide some mental organisation for the frequent confusion of political life.[45]

Test of Survival

It may be said that all ideologies must meet the test of survival on the following major points.

1. Ideologies must meet the test of creating institutions adequate to ensure their domestic survival in the group of origin.[46] The ideology is the system.[47] It makes the institutions work to fit it.[48] It is due to this that in a liberal—democratic country ideology is a very flexible affair which always remains subject to challenge and revision. Contrary to this, in a totalitarian country, it becomes ruthless, it creates a single centre, a one-party elite, a terror, an all pervasive and controlling espionage system, and periodic purges.[49]
2. In turn institutions depend on ideas—rigid for totalitarian myths, revisable for free societies.[50] It is due to this that while the progress of democracy sees more and more reform of the parliament, extension of suffrage, increase in the scope of state activity towards general welfare and the live, all showing change in the premises of liberal ideology by virtue of its ever remaining subject to the course of revision.[51] But a totalitarian ideology has a more or less fixed character.[52] There is very little ambivalence in it.[53] Moreover, it all leads first to the cultivation of some 'magic formula' and then its conversion into a religion.[54]
3. Ideologies must meet the test of the survival not only interms of truth, but also in those of power, *i.e.*, in conflict with other systems.[55] In a sense, the test of

survival depends upon the psychological impact that it makes on the people.[56] Instead of pessimism there should be optimism so that the people may be convinced of something good after the defeat or extermination of the evil.[57] Challenge of the opponent should be countered with a sense of hope.[58] In simple terms, it implies that the ideology of liberalism should reshape itself so as to convience the people with the survival of democracy in the world in the face of all devastating challenges of totalitarianism.[59]

4. Ideologies must meet the condition of economic inadequacy.[60] Indeed, this is the test by which communism, condemns its rivals and justifies its own superiority.[61] It poses the supreme test of so perfect an economic system, brought about by the suppression of all classes and class war and the control of the instruments of production in the hands of the dictatorship of the proletariat, that the state can wither away and the economic order would be carried on with anarchic freedom.[62] In opposition to this, the ideology of capitalism thrives on the boons of economic liberty leading to the production and distribution of more goods to the consumers who are free to express their wants and join the world of free competition.[63]

5. The final and ultimate test of any ideology is its hold on men's souls.[64] Whereas communism proposes no other end or goal of human freedom than 'from each according to his ability, to each according to his need.[65] Liberalism postulates that 'man lives by liberty alone'.[66] The line of fundamental difference between the two may be discovered in the fact that while the former manages to establish its hold on the minds of the people by means of force, the latter has the same by their free acceptance.[67]

REFERENCES

1. Watkins, The Age of Ideology (Englewood Cliffs, New Jersey : Prentice Hall, 1964), p. 106.
2. See Drucker, The Political Uses of Ideology (London : Macmillan, 1974), p. 3.
3. Frank Thakurdas, "The Expanding Frontier of Political Science" in Indian Journal of Political Science, Vol. XXXIV, No. 4, 1973, p. 415.
4. H.D. Aiken, The Age of Ideology, pp. 16-17.
5. C.B. Macpherson, Democratic Theory : Essays in Retrieval, Oxford : Clarendon Press, 1975, pp. 157-58.
6. See Carl J. Friedrich and B.K. Brzezinski, Totalitarian Dictatorship and Autocracy (New York, 1965), p. 88.
7. S.E. Finer, Comparative Government (London : Allen Lane, The Penguin Press, 1970), p. 43.
3. See Preston King and B. Parekh (eds.), Politics and Experience (Cambridge, 1969), p. 351.
9. A.R. Ball, Modern Politics and Government (London : Macmillan, 1971), p. 256.
10. See Daniel Bell, End of Ideoloy : On the Exhaustion of Political Ideas in the Fifties (New York, 1968), pp. 393-404.
11. K. Seshadri, Studies on Marxism and Political Science, (New Delhi : People's Pub., 1977), p. 193.
12. R.K. Dahl, Modern Political Analysis (Englewood Cliffs, New Jersey : Prentice Hall, 1976), p. 61.
13. R.E. Lane, Political Ideology (New York : Free Press, 1962), pp. 14-15.
14. Aron, "The Diffusion of Ideologies" in Stankiewicz, p. 45.
15. Raymond Aron, The opium of the Intellectuals (London, 1957), p. 324.
16. Aron, Democracy and Totalitarianism (London, 1956), p. 236.
17. See Eric Hoffer, The True Believer : Thoughts on the Nature Mass Movements (New York, 1951).
18. F.W. Coker, "Some Present Day Critics of Liberalism" in Stankiewicz, *op. cit.*, p. 379.

19. Spengler, The Hour of Decision, Translated from German into English by Charlies Francis Atkins (New York, 1934), p. 119.
20. S.P. Huntington, Conservatism as an Ideology, Stankiewicz, *op. cit.*, p. 359.
21. *Ibid.*, p. 358.
22. *Ibid.*, p. 360.
23. *Ibid.*, *op. cit.*, p. 375.
24. W.H. Greenleaf, Oakeshotts' Philosophical Politics (London : Longmans,1966), p. 46.
25. Drucker, *op. cit.*, p. 117.
26. See Plamenatz, Ideology (London, 1970), pp. 50ff.
27. See Marx-Engles, Collected Works, Vol. IV, p. 480.
28. Engels, Select Correspondence, p. 421.
29. Marx, The German Ideology, p. 37.
30. Michael Evans, Karl Marx (London : George Allen and Unwin, 1975), p. 83.
31. *Ibid.*
32. Marx, Capital, Vol. I, p. 761.
33. Evans, *op. cit.*, p. 83.
34. Marx, Engles, Collected Works, Vol. III, p. 46.
35. A.R. Ball, Modern Politics and Government (London Macmillan, 1971), p. 257.
36. Mannheim, Ideology and Utopia (London, 1936), p. 143.
37. Drucker, *op. cit.*, p. 20.
38. *Ibid.*, p. 21.
39. Mannheim, *op. cit.*, p. 184.
40. Drucker, *op. cit.*, p. 21.
41. See Lasswell and Kaplan, Power and Society (New Haven : Yale Univ., Press, 1950), Chapters 3 and 6.
42. Drucker, *op. cit.*, p. 22.
43. V.P. Varma, Political Philosophy (Agra : Lakshmi Narain, 1970), p. 93.

44. Randhir Singh, Reason, Revolution and Political Theory, (New Delhi : People's Pub. House, 1976), p. XVI.
45. Dobb, On Economic Theory and Socialism (London, 1955), p. 233.
46. C.J. Friedrich and B.K. Brezezinski, "Types of Totalitarian Ideology" in Stankiewicz, *op. cit.*, p. 48.
47. Talcott Parsons, The Social System (New York : Free Press of Glencoe, 1951), p. 349.
48. Friedrich and Brzezinski, "The General Charcteristics of Totalitarian Dictatorship" in Stankiewicz, *op. cit.*, p. 40.
49. Friedrich and Brzezinski, "Types of Totalitarian Ideology", *op. cit.*, p. 46.
50. Lenin, Selected Works, Vol. VII, p. 24.
51. Stalin, Problems of Leninism, p. 659 ff.
52. Marx, Capital, Vol. I, pp. 23-24.
53. Finer, *op. cit.*, p. 88.
54. E. Nolte, Three Faces of Fascism (London, 1956), pp. 20-21.
55. F.W. Coker, Recent Political Thought (New York : Appleton Century, 1934), pp. 482-83.
56. Martin Seliger, The Marxist Conception of Ideology, (London : Cambridge Univ., Press, 1977), p. 1.
57. *Ibid., op. cit.*, pp. 45-47.
58. *Ibid., op. cit.*, pp. 48-50.
59. *Ibid., op. cit.*, pp. 52-56.
60. *Ibid., op. cit.*, pp. 57-58.
61. *Ibid., op. cit.*, pp. 59-60.
62. See Dante Germino, Beyond Ideology : The Revival of Political Theory (New York : Harper, 1967), p. 167.
63. *Ibid.*, p. 199.
64. *Ibid.*, p. 200.
65. Seshadri, *op. cit.*, pp. 190-91.
66. Varma, *op. cit.*, p. 93.
67. Drucker, *op. cit.*, p. 141.

(C) THE DEMOCRATIC IDEAL

One of the most striking features of contemporary politics is the astonishing popularity of democracy.[1] There are few people now-a-days, whether major political leaders or ordinary citizens and subjects, who do not praise democracy and claim to be democrats. Except for fascists, Nazis and a few others, infact, everyone seems to agree that democracy is desirable. Many people use the word "democracy" in a hypocritical or deceptive way. Democracy is so popular, in other words, that everyone will try to link his or her ideology. Perhaps, there is a genuine and widespread agreement that democracy is the true end or goal of ideological activity, with disagreement arising only over the proper means for achieving that end. Democracy like freedom, is an essentially contested concept. The democratic ideal is itself deeply involved in the ideological conflict of the modern world. To understand this conflict, we need to know more about democracy and the democratic ideal.[2]

The Origins of Democracy

"Democracy" the word and democracy the form of political life both began in ancient Greece.[3] The word comes from a combination of the Greek noun demos, meaning "people" or "common people", and the verb kratein, to rule. For the Greeks, demokratia meant specifically rule or government by the common people—That is, those who were uneducated, unsophisticated and poor. Because these people made up the majority of the citizenry, democracy was identified, as it often is today, with majority rule.

The centre of activity in ancient Greece, which was not united under a single government, was the self governing polis, or city state. Athens, the largest polis provides the best example of a democratic city-state. Throughout most of the second half of the fifth century B.C., the period renowned as the "Golden Age of Athenians" called their polis a democracy. Not everyone willingly accepted this state of affairs, but those who did seem to have embraced democracy enthusiastically. Even more significantly Athenian democracy was another aspect of their notion of citizenship. To be a citizen, one had to be an adult, free, male Athenian. Women, resident foreigners, and slaves (who may have made up a majority of the population) were all excluded. In fact, only about one out of ten inhabitants of Athens was a citizen. From the vantage point of the late twentieth century, then, it appears that Athenian democracy was hardly democratic at all.

The Athenian Assembly sometimes banished citizens temporarily from Athens, without trial and even without legal charges being brought against them, simply because the majority of the Assembly thought these citizens posed a danger to the polis. Sometimes the punishment for voicing unpopular views was even harsher. We know this especially from the case of Socrates (469-399 B.C.), the philosopher was tried, convicted and condemned to death by poision on the ground of religious impiety and corrupting the morals of the youth of Athens.[4] Further, in the fourth and fifth centuries B.C., however, democracy faced a different criticism. This was the complaint that democracy is a dangerously unstable form of government. Foremost among those who made this complaint was Socrates student and friend, Plato (427-347 B.C.)

Plato believed that democracy is dangerous, because it puts political power into the hands of ignorant and envious people. Because they are ignorant, he argued, the people will not know how to use political power for the common good. Because they are envious they will be concerned only with their own good, which they will seek to advance by plundering those who are better off. Because they are both ignorant and envious, they will be easily swayed by demagogues—literally, leaders of the demos—who will flatter them, appeal to their envy, and turn citizen against citizen. From democracy, in short, comes civil war and anarchy, the destruction of the city-state. When democracy has left the 'polis' in this wretched condition, according to Plato's analysis, the people will cry out for law and order.[5] They will then rally around anyone strong enough to bring an end to anarchy. But such a person will be a despot. Plato said a tyrant who cares nothing about the polis or the people because he cares only for power. So from democracy, rule by the people, it is but a series of short steps to despotism.

Plato (427-347 B.C.)

This argument against democracy found favour with a number of political thinkers, including Plato's student Aristotle (384-322 B.C.). Aristotle maintained that democracy is one of six basic kinds of political regimes or constitutions. Governing power, he said in his politics, must be in the hands of one person, a few people, or many, and this power may be exercised either for the good of the whole community in which case it is good or true—or solely for the good of the rulers—in which case it is bad or perverted. By combining these features, Aristotle arrived at the six cell scheme illustrated in the figure.

		In whose interest?	
		Public	Self
Rule by	One	Monarchy	Tyranny
	The Few	Aristocracy	Oligarchy
	The many	Polity	Democracy
		"True"	"Perverted"

The features of Aristotle's classification of regimes are especially noteworthy. The first, of course is that he followed Plato in considering democracy to be bad or undesirable. For Aristotle, democracy is a corrupt form of rule because the demos tends to be shortsighted and selfish. The common people will recklessly pursue their own interests by taking poverty, wealth, and power from the few with no regard for the peace and stability of the polis as a whole. But this serves their interests only in the short run, and in the end they will bring chaos, and ultimately despotism, on the whole polis.

The second noteworthy feature of Aristotle's classification is the inclusion of polity, a good form of rule by the many. For Aristotle, polity differs from democracy because it mixes elements of rule by the few with elements of rule by the many. In a democracy, that is, the many will be poor. He said most of the people are neither rich nor poor.

One can expect the many to rule in a prudent manner. This is because the many, when they are "middle class", will avoid the excesses of the envious poor and the arrogant rich. If the middle class rule, there will be moderation, peace and stability in the city state.[7]

Aristotle (384-322 B.C.)

In the final analysis, Aristotle believed polity to be good—he even suggested that it is the best of the six regimes while democracy is bad. But he argued that democracy is better than tyranny and oligarchy. This is because many heads are better Judges than one or a few. Even if none of the common people is an especially good Judge of what is right or wrong, good or bad, beautiful or ugly, their collective Judgement is still better than that of any individual or small group, including a group of experts.

Niccolo Machiavelli (1469-1527)

In the late Middle Ages, particularly in the thirteenth century. Several developments prepared the way for the Renaissance (or "rebirth")[8]. During this Age, rebirth or revival that began in the Italian city-states. Machiavelli

(1469-1527) was a prominent official in the Republic of florence in 1512 when the medici family overthrew the republican government and installed themselves as rulers of the city state. Implicated in the plot of overthrow the medici and restore the republic, Machiavelli was arrested, tortured, and banished to his family estate in the countryside. When in exile, he wrote two books—the prince and the discourses. He said republican form of government is the best.

In Britain, the turmoil of the 1600s sparked interest in both republicanism and democracy. During the English Civil war of the 1640's some supporters of the parliamentary cause took the radial position of advocating democracy.

Democracy as an Ideal

To say that democracy is an ideal means that it is something forward which people aim or aspire. Despite the difficulties of refining it, the democratic ideal of "rule by the people" remains popular. This is due in part to its connection with freedom and quality, since democracy implies that in some sense every citizen will be both free and equal to every other. Whether we accept or reject it, all ideologies must come to terms with the democratic ideal.

The Conceptions of Democracy

To clarify the connection between political ideologies and the democratic ideal, let us examine briefly the three principal versions of democracy in the twentieth century.

1. Liberal Democracy

As the name suggests, liberal democracy emerged from liberalism. As with liberalism in general, liberal democracy stresses the rights and liberty of the individual.[9] For liberals, democracy is certainly rule by the people, but an essential part of this rule includes the protection of individual rights and liberties. This means that majority rule must be limited.

Democracy is rule by the majority of the people, in this view, but only as long as those in the majority do not try to deprive individuals of their basic civil rights. The right to speak and worship freely, the right to run for public office, the right to own property—these are among the civil rights and liberties that liberals have generally taken to be necessary to realise the democratic ideal as they interpret it.[10]

2. Social Democracy

Within the western democracies, especially in Europe, the chief challenger to the liberal conception is social democracy. This view is linked to the ideology of socialism. From a "social democratic" or "democratic socialist" perspective, the key to democracy is equality, especially equal power in society and government. Social democrats argue that liberal democracy puts poor and working class people at the mercy of the rich. In the modern world, they say money is a major source of power, and those who have wealth have power over those who do not. So, the rich exercise much greater influence when public policies are made. Democracy is rule by the people, and such rule requires that every person have a roughly equal influence over the government. This is in keeping with the slogan, "One person, one vote" like liberals, then, social democrats want to preserve civil liberaties and promote fair competition for political office.[11]

3. People's Democracy

In communist countries, the prevailing version of the democratic ideal has been people's democracy. In some ways, people's democracy is closer to the original Greek idea of democracy. From a communist perspective, the common people are the proletariat or the working class, and democracy will not be achieved until government rules in their interest.[12]

Conclusion

Liberal democracy, social democracy and people's democracy are the main visions of the democratic ideal in the modern world. In this democratic age, it is important to understand these visions and how they relate to various political ideologies.

REFERENCES

1. Plato, Apology, 31, In the Trial and Death of Socrates Trans. G.M.A., Grube (Indianapolis : Hackett Publishing Company 1983), p. 33.
2. For Plato's account of democracy, See book VIII of the Republic.
3. Benjamin Jowett, ed. and trans., The Politics of Aristotle (New York : Modern Library, 1943), p. 192; also in Ball and Dagger, eds., Ideals and Ideologies, selection 4.
4. *Ibid., op. cit.,* pp. 146, Ideals and Ideologies, Selection 4.
5. William Shakespeare, King Henry, The Six, Third Part, Act III, selection 2.
6. See, *e.g.,* Mary Dietz, "Trapping the Prince : Machiavelli and the Politics of Deception, "American Political Science Review 80 (September 1986) : 777-799.
7. The Federalist Papers, No. 51.
8. Dahl, Robert, Democracy and Its Critics. New Haven, CT : Yale University Press, 1989.
9. Dunn, John, ed., Democracy : The Unfinished Journey, Oxford : Oxford University Press, 1992.
10. Held, David, Models of Democracy Stanford, CA : Standford University Press, 1986.
11. Skinner, Quentin, The Foundations of Modern Political Thought, 2 vols., Cambridge : Cambridge University Press, 1978.
12. Walzer, Michael, Radical Principles, New York : Basic Books, 1981.

2

CONSERVATISM

In one sense conservatism is easy to define, in another quite difficult. It is easy because all conservatives share desire to "conserve" or preserve something—usually the traditional or customary way of life of their societies.[1] But these traditions or customs are likely to vary considerably from one society to another. Different conservatives are likely to have different ideas about what elements or parts of their established way of life are worth preserving conservatives may all want to conserve something, then but they do not all want to conserve the same things. And that is what makes conservatism so difficult to define.[2]

The founder of conservatism was Edmund Burke (1729-1797), an Irishman who moved to England and served for nearly 30 years in the House of Commons of the British Parliament.[3] Burke never called himself a conservative–neither "conservatism" nor "Liberalism" entered the vocabulary of politics until the 1800s-–but in his speeches and writings he defined a distinctively "conservative" political position.

Burke developed and expounded his views in the heat of political controversies, particularly in reaction to the French Revoluton.[4] When the revolution began in 1788 and 1789, many observers in England hailed it as a great step forward for both France and the cause of liberty. But Burke saw the French Revolution, from the beginning, as a foolhardy attempt to create a new society from the ground up.[5]

Edmund Burke (1729–1797)

Burke objection to the French Revolution rests largely on the claim that the revolutionaries misunderstood human nature. Burke said, political society is no mere heap of individuals, but a living and changing organism, a whole that is greater than the sum of its parts. 'On this organic view, individuals are related to society in the same way that the heart and eyes and arms are related to the body—not a separate and isolated units, but as interdependent members of a living organism. Burke said society is like fabric—the "social fabric"—and its individual members are like the interwoven threads. Burke said, social or political society rests on a contract, it is no ordinary contract between individuals, but a sacred covenent that binds whole generations together. Society is nothing but a partnership in all science, a partnership in all art, a partnership in every virtue, and in all perfection. As the ends of such a partnership cannot be obtained in many generations, it becomes a partnership not only between those who are living, but between those who are living, those who are dead, and those who are to be born.[7]

To preserve this partnership, Burke believed that both government and long standing customs and traditions are indispensable. People tend to be self-interested and short sighted, which is precisely why they need the power of government to restrain them and to keep their passions in check.[8] But government is not something that can be taken apart and resembled whenever and however people want. It is a complex and delicate organism that must be rooted in the customs and traditions of the people, who must acquire the habit of obeying, respecting, and even revering[9] it.

For Burke and classical conservatives, liberty is worthwhile only when it is properly ordered.[10] Individuals should be free from obstacles to pursue their goals, but only when their goals do not threaten the social order, if they do, then their freedom must be restricted.

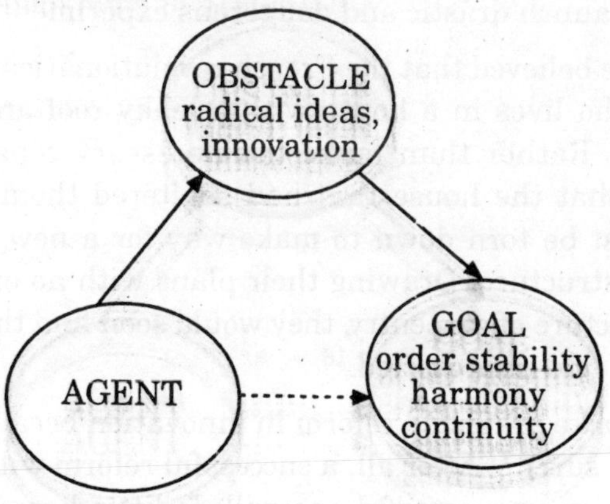

Burke was not opposed to all revolutions. He looked back with approval to England's "Glorious Revolution" of 1688, and as a member of parliament he was sympathetic to the American Colonies in their struggle with the British Government.[11] But in Burke's view these were revolutions in the old fashioned sense. According to Burke, then, the English and Americans had fought to restore their rights, to return to a condition they had previously enjoyed. But the French were engaged in a revolution of a new and much more radical sort. The sought to uproot the settled order of their society and government in order to replace it with something new and untried and therefore certain, Burke believed, to end, in disaster.[12]

Burke never claimed that French government and society were perfect, nor did he flatly oppose any and all attempts at change.[13] On the contrary, he regarded change as a necessary feature of human life and society. But change should be brought about carefully and gradually—the kind of change that Burke called reform—and not through innovation. As he saw it, innovation is the attempt to do something new or novel on the grounds that the new must be better than the old.[14] Innovation is therefore change for the sake of change, based on abstract reason. In abandons the old ways, the habits that have stood the test of time, in order to launch drastic and dangerous experiments.[15]

Burke believed that the French revolutionaries were like people who lives in a house with a leaky roof and broken windows. Rather than make the necessary repairs, they decided that the house that had sheltered them all their lives must be torn down to make way for a new, glorious, rational structure. Drawing their plans with no experience of architecture of carpentry, they would soon find themselves homeless and unprotected.[16]

So Burke preferred reform in innovation because it was safer and surer.[17] After all, a successful reform will do some good and an unsuccessful one will do little harm. He also claimed that reform grew out of prejudice, which he thought superior to abstract reason. Burke claimed, prejudice is stored up or "latent wisdom". Customs and traditions have gradually evolved over the generations, so they reflect the lessons that people and societies have learned, bit by bit, in the course of their lives.[18] The fact is that traditions have lasted so long is evidence that they have literally stood the test of time. They embody the wisdom not just of one or two people, but of generations.

Edmund Burke died 1799. And he is often called the father of conservatism.

Conservatism as an Ideology

With all the division and diversity within the conservative camp, does it still make sense to speak of conservatism as a single ideology.[19] In our view it does. For one thing, conservatives are no more divided among themselves than the followers of other ideologies. For another, the differences that distinguish the several varieties of conservatism from one another should not obscure certain "family resemblances" they all share.[20] These can be classified by considering how conservatism performs the four functions of all ideologies : the explanatory, evaluative, orientative, and programmatic functions.[21]

1. *Explanation :* For most conservatives, the basis for explaining why social conditions are the way they are is human imperfection. Conservatives do refer to other factors historical circumstances and economic conditions, for instance, and certainly government policies and cultural trends but they ultimately trace all these to the frailty of imperfect human nature.[22] If things have gone wrong, it is probably because fallible men and women, acting through government have tried to do more than humans are capable of doing. If things have gone well, it is because they have kept their hopes and expectations low and proceeded with caution.[23]

2. *Evaluation* : But how do we know when things have gone well or poorly? Conservatives usually evaluate social conditions, by appealing to social peace and stability. If relations between the different classes or levels of society are harmonious, so that the leaders display a sense of responsibility to the followers and the followers a sense of loyalty to the leaders, then the social fabric is in good condition. If it is torn by conflict, strife, and bitterness, however then action must be taken to repair the fraying social fabric.[24]

3. *Orientation* : Conservatism tells the individual that he or she is not simply an individual. Each of us is part of a greater whole, and each should realise that he or she must act with the good of the whole society in mind. The best way to do this usually to play our part in society—to be a good parent or teacher or engineer or plumber—and to recognize how each part must blend with all others to provide social harmony.[25]

4. *Programme* : The political programme that conservatives pursue varies from one time and place to another. But the general message of conservatives is to take things slowly, proceed carefully, on the grounds that it is better to do a little good than a lot of harm.[26] In gazing towards the possibilities of a glorious future, conservatives point out, it is all too easy to lose sight of the good things we already enjoy. We should take our eyes off distant horizons in order to appreciate the scenery that surrounds us. Once we see this clearly, conservatives say, we will cherish and conserve it.[27]

REFERENCES

1. Peter Viereck, Conservatism : From John Adams to Churchill (New York : Van Nostrand Reinhold 1956), p. 19.
2. Anthony Quinton, The Politics of Imperfection (London : Faber and Faber, 1978).

3. Peter Viereck, Conservatism Revisited (New York : Collier Books, 1962), p. 35. See also William Golding's novel, Lord of the Flies (1954).
4. Robert Bork, Stouching Towards Gomorrah : Modern Liberalism and American Decline (New York : Harper Collins, 1996), p. 21.
5. Issac Kramnick and Frederick Watkins, The Age of Ideology : 1750 to the present, 2nd ed. (Englewood Cliffs, NJ : Prentice-Hall, 1979), p. 270.
6. Reflections on the Revolution in France, ed. Conor Cruise O'Brien (Harmondworth Penguin, 1968), pp. 194-195, See also Terence Ball and Richard Dagger, ed., Ideals and Ideologies : A Reader, 3rd ed., (New York : Longman, 1919), Selection 24.
7. *Ibid.*, p. 91.
8. Roger Scruton, The Meaning of Conservatism (London : Macmillan, 1984), p. 19.
9. In Hanna Pitkin, ed., Representation (New York : Atherton, 1969), pp. 174-175.
10. Jack Lively, ed., The Works of Joseph de Maistre (New York : Macmillan, 1965), p. 78, also in Ideals and Ideologies, Selection 25.
11. In Viereck, Conservatism, pp. 165-166.
12. *Ibid.,* p. 44.
13. Ball and Dagger, eds., Ideals and Ideologies, Selection 27.
14. *Ibid., op. cit.,* pp. 48.
15. Garry Wills, Confessions of a Conservative, (Garden city, NY : Doubleday, 1979).
16. See the essays in Oakeshott's Rationalism in Politics (London : Methuen, 1962), Most of the latter essay is included in Ball and Dagger, eds., Ideals and Ideologies, Selection 28.
17. George Will, Statecraft as Soulcraft : What Government Does (New York : Simon and Schuster, 1983, pp. 119-120).
18. Irving Kristol, Two Cheers for Capitalism (New York : Basic Books, 1978).

19. Daniel Bell, The Cultural Contradictions of Capitalism (New York : Basic Books, 1976).
20. Irving Kristol, "Family Values—Not a Political Issue", Wall Street Journal (December 7, 1992), pp. 45.
21. Ralph Reed, Politically Incorrect, (Dallas, IX : World Publishing, 1994), pp. 35-36.
22. O Gorman, Frank, Edmund Burke : His Political Philosophy, London : Allen and Unwin, 1973.
23. Kirk Russel, The Conservative Mind : From Burke to Eliot, 4th *ed.,* New York : Avon Books, 1968 p. 48.
24. *Ibid., op. cit.,* pp. 50.
25. *Ibid., op. cit.,* pp. 55-60.
26. Rossiter, Clinton Conservatism in America : The Thankless Persuasion, 2nd ed., New York : Random House, 1962, pp. 65-70.
27. Hogg, Quintin, The Case for Conservatism, Harmondsworth : Penguin, 1947.

3

SOCIALISM

Introduction

Modern socialism, like classical conservatism, began in part as a critique of the liberalism of the late eighteenth and nineteenth centuries.[1] Like the conservatives, socialists objected to the liberal emphasis on self-interest, competition, and individual liberty. For socialists believed then, as now that human beings are by nature social or communal creatures. Individuals do not live or work or reproduce the species in isolation, but in co-operation with another.[2] It is co-operation among individuals, not competition between them, that socialists see as the foundation of a society in which everyone can enjoy a decent measure of liberty, justice, and prosperity.[3]

But socialists, unlike classical conservatives, assign no particular value to tradition or custom. Nor do they share the conservatives fondness for private property. From the socialist viewpoint, infact, private property is the source of the class divisions that place some people in positions of power and privilege while condemning others to poverty and powerlessness. Indeed, socialists usually class for programmes that will distribute wealth and power more evenly throughout society–programmes that conservatives typically deplore as social product, and everyone who participates in producing a good is entitled to a share in it. This means that society as a whole, and not private individuals should own and control property for the benefit of all. This is the fundamental conviction that all socialists share.[4]

But what exactly does this mean? How much property is society to own and control? To this question different socialists have responded in very different ways. Some suggest that most goods should be regarded as public property, others maintain that only the major means of production—such as rivers, and forest, large factories and mines—should be publicly owned and controlled.[5]

This raises a second question : How is society to exercise this control? It is one thing to say that society as a whole should own and control a power plant. Some socialists argued for centralized and some decentralized control of public property. Those who favour centralised control want to see the state or government assume the responsibility for managing property and resources in the name of the whole society. This was the approach followed by the Soviet Union. Other socialists, dispute this claim by pointing to the top-heavy and sluggish bureaucracies that dominate centrally planned economies. But those who favour decentralised, they believes in the distribution of power in every society. Poor people have a good deal less power than the rich the less power because they have leps ability to control and direct their own lives and to choose where and how to live.[6]

SOCIALISM : THE PRECURSORS

The first name one associates with the ideology of socialism. Plato's Republic (380 B.C.) presents one early version, although plato restricted the communal sharing of goods and spouses in his ideal society to a particular class, the guardians. Utopian thinkers such as Sir, Thomas More, (1478-1535) the catholic saint and martyr of the early sixteenth century, advocated communal ownership as an antidote to the sins of pride, envy and greed policies that encouraged competition for profit also encouraged these sins, more chared. As a result, most people were poor and powerless, while a few became rich and powerful. And even these few who gained material wealth paid a price, as their pursuit of money and position left them morally and spiritually improverished. "Wherever men have private property and money is the measure of everything." The principal character of More's Utopia (1516) says "there it is hardly possible for the commonwealth to be governed. Justly or to flourish in prosperity. No equal and just distribution of goods can be made unless private property is outlawed and banished.[7] And in Utopia, it is. Money is abolished. Once the fear of poverty and hunger and homelessness are banished, the foundations of greed and envy disappear.

1. Saint Simon

One of the first to try to set socialism on a "Scientific" basis was the French aristocrat, Saint Simon (1760-1825). Human history, he held is divided into successive stages or periods.[8] As an older form of society disappears, a new one necessarily arises to take its place. Each is marked by the presence of particular classes and depends upon certain beliefs. As these beliefs lose credibility, so too does the social and economic system that rests upon them.[9] Thus, said Saint-Simon, feudal society was marked by the presence of a landed nobility and a clergy who articulated the religious assumptions and beliefs upon which feudalism rested. These were in turn undermined and eventually replaced by the enlightenment and the coming of industrial society, with its emphasis on science and technology. A new class of scientists, engineers, and industrialists was being increasingly important, said Saint-Simon, because without them, there could be no industrial society.[10] This new form of society was enormously complex, depending as it did on the co-ordinated knowledge of skills of many different types of technicians and expects. In such a society it made no sense to speak, as liberals did, of "the individuals". The isolated individual is a fiction. In the red world of the industrial society, individuals are reduced to their social roles and productive functions.[11] Through planning, simon declared experts could anticipate and thus meet social needs, providing an economic system that was both more efficient and more just than capitalism.

Carrying this idea further still, Simon's disciple August Comte (1798-1857) called himself a "positive" and emphasized the importance of scientific planning, prediction and social control.[12] "From Science" he said, "comes prevision, from prevision comes control. With its emphasis on social control, Comte's "Positivist". Version of socialism was characterised by a deep aversion to democracy and a fondness for technocracy, or rule by experts. Like Simon, Comte equated socialism with systematic "scientific" social planning which was in turn to be justified by a new "religion of humanity" in which scientists were to be the high priests and the Comte the Pope.[13]

Although Simon and Comte favoured centralized control of social production, other socialists in the early 1800s took the opposite position. Two prominent proponents of a decentralist version of socialism were Charles Fourier and Robert Owen, both of whom inspired disciples to establish short lived Utopian Communities in the U.S.A.[14] Fourier and Owen devised schemes for a socialist society that were as visionary as Saint-Simon's and Comte's, but their visions were of small, self sufficient, self-governing communities in which decisions were made not by experts, but by all adult members of the community.[15]

2. Fourier

Charles Fourier (1772-1837) was a French Socialist whose vision of utopia derived from a mixture of mysticism, numerology, and a crude psychological theory. Modern society he said, is not so far from barbarism as its inhabitants are inclined to believe.[16] It is afflicted with the evils of commerce, selfishness, and deception, among many others. We not only deceive others, we also deceive ourselves by holding false or mistaken beliefs—especially the belief that wealth will bring happiness. The evils of commercial society, with its mad pursuit of wealth, are embodied in its institutions.[17] The institutions of marriage, the male-dominated family, and the competitive market prevent the satisfaction of the passions, which are twelve in number. These include the passions of the five senses, along with those of familism, friendship, love, and ambition, to these added the "butterfly" passion that leads us to look for variety, the "cabalistic" passion for plotting and intrigue, and the "composite"[18] passion for combining physical and mental pleasures. There is also a thirteenth, the passion for "harmony" that comes from the proper balance of the basic passions. But a competitive commercial society frustrates our desire for harmony, Fourier insisted. We can never satisfy this passion when we are divided against each other and against ourselves—by competition for jobs and profits.[19] Only when the evils of this society are overcome will humanity reach its highest stage. "Harmonism", in which human beings will co-operate freely for the common good.

Fourier's vision of a harmonies society was captured in his account of the "phalanstery" a community of about 1,600–1,610—the ideal population—he said in which the residents would produce all they needed and all the passions would be fully satisfied.[20] The phalanstery was based on the principle of "attractive labour", which held that people will work voluntarily if only they find on occupation that engages their talents and interests. Those who like to grow things will be the gardeners. Those who like children will provide day care.[21] And children, who are like to play in the dirt, will sweep the streets and collect the garbage. Because people will work freely and spontaneously in these circumstances, the coercive apparatus of the state—laws, police, courts, prisons—will not be needed. Socialist society as Fourier envisioned it, will be productive, prosperous, and free.[22]

3. Owen

Robert Owen (1771-1857) was a British capitalist who, became an ardent socialist. Drunkenness, debauchery, theft, and other evils were, he held, the result not of original sin or of individual character defects, but of a deformed social system. By rewarding greed and selfishness of the capitalist, the capitalist system sent the wrong message to young people.[23] Little wonder, then, that so many people try to advance themselves at other people's expense. The cure for the evils of capitalism can be found not only in a new system of production co-operative production for public profit—but in a new system of education as well. Owen believed that deformed character was the result of defective education where "education" is understood in the broadest possible sense at the sum of all the formative influences in one's life.

In 1800 in New Lanark, Scotland Owen established a model textile factory that was radical by the standards of the day. The factory was clean and working conditions were relatively safe. The work week was reduced. Children under ten were not only allowed to work, but were educated at the Owner's expense. Besides learning the Three Rs. children learned the value and necessity of co-operation in all aspects of life.[24]

Over the next ten years, Owen laboured tirelessly to persuade his fellow capitalists to see the merits of his scheme. He also appealed to workers to share his vision of a network of small, self-sufficient communities that would spread around the globe. He was more successful with the latter than with the former, who were understandably worried by Owen's attacks on private property and religion and his growing popularity among the working class.[25] In 1824 Owen took his ideas to North America. On 30,000 acres, he had purchased in southwest Indiana, he established the Socialist Community of New Harmony, which he intended as a model of social organization. Within four years, however, New Harmony had failed, and Owen lost most of his fortune in the venture. He spent the remainder of his life promoting trade unionism and advocating the establishment of worker owned cooperatives as the nucleus from which a larger and more comprehensive socialist society might grow.[26]

THE SOCIALISM OF MARX
Karl Marx (1818-1883)

1. Marx Theory of History

Like Hegel, Marx saw history as the story of human labour and struggle. Humans have had to struggle to survive heat and cold and the ever-present threat of starvation in order to wrest a living from a recalcitrant nature.[27] But human beings have struggled against each other. Historically, the most important of these conflicts are to be found in the struggle of one class against another. "The history of all hitherto existing society," write Marx and Engels in the communist manifesto, "is the history of class struggles". Different classes masters and slaves in slave societies, Lords and Serfs in feudal society, and later capitalists and workers in capitalist society have different interests, aims, and aspirations.[28] Their interests were opposed to each other. So long as societies are divided into different classes, class conflict is inevitable.

2. Materialistic Conception of History

Marx called materialistic conception of history "the leading thread in my studies." Marx called his interpretation of history materialist to distinguish it from of spirit's self realization, Marx saw history as the story of class struggles over opposing material, or economic, interests and resources. This does not mean that Marx was, as has sometimes been charged, an "economic determinist" who wished to "reduce everything to economics."[29] He did, however, emphasis the primary importance of material production. "Before men do anything else," he said, "they must first produce the means of their subsistence"—the food they eat, the clothing they wear, the houses they live in, and so on. Everything else, Marx held, follows from the necessity to produce the material means of our subsistence.

Karl Marx (1818–1883)

Material production requires two things. First, it requires what Marx called the material forces of production. These will vary from one kind of society to another. In primitive hunting society, for example, the forces of production include the wild game, the hunter's bow, arrows, knives and other tools.[30] In somewhat more Sophisticated agrarian society, the forces of production include the seeds to be planted, the hoes or other implements used in planting and harvesting the crops, and the tools employed in separating the wheat from the chaff, milling the grain, baking the bread and so on. And in a still more sophisticated industrial society, the productive forces include raw materials (metallic ores, coal, wood, petroleum and so on), machinery for extracting these materials from their natural state, the factories in which these materials are turned into commodities, the freight cars and trucks for transporting raw materials to the factories and finished products to markets and the like.[31]

Friedrich Engels (1820–1895)

In addition to raw materials and machinery—the forces of production—material production requires a second factor that Marx called "the social relations of production". Human beings organise themselves in order to extract the raw materials to invent make, operate, and repair the machinery, to build and staff the factories, and so on.[32] The social relations of production or social relations or social formations are of different types says Marx. A hunting society, for example, will have hunters almost always the younger males—who are organised into hunting parties, the females who bear and raise the children and transform the hides into clothing, blankets and other useful items, and others with still other tasks to perform. In an agricultural society, the social relations of production include those who make the tools who shoe and harness the horses, who plant the seeds and harvest the crop, who winnow the grain, who grind or mill it, and who bake the bread. The social relations of production in an industrial society are even more complex. They include the miners who extract the ore, the lumberjacks who fell the trees, the railway workers who transport raw materials to the factory, the people who invent, build, operate and repair the machines, the bankers and brokers who raise the capital and the investors who invest it, and many others.[33]

Out of these social relations of production the different classes arise. We can simplify somewhat by imaging any society to contain two antagonistic classes, one of which dominates the other. A slave society has a dominant class of masters and a subservient class of slaves.[34] In feudal society, the two contending classes are the feudal lords and their serfs. And in an industrial capitalist society these classes and the capitalists and the wage-labourers. Which class you belong to depend upon your relation to the forces of production. Very roughly, you belong to the subservient class if you are yourself merely a means or a force of production. And if you own or control the forces of production-including human forces then you belong to the dominant class. Less roughly and more precisely, you belong to the subservient or working class if you do not own but are infact, forced to transfer your labour or "labour power" to another for his or her pleasure or profit.[35]

In every class-divided society, Marx notes, the dominant class tends to be much smaller than the dominated class. Slaves outnumber masters, serfs outnumber feudal lords, and workers outnumber capitalists. But the ruling class is powerful, because it controls the agents and agencies of coercion—the police, courts, prisons and other institutions of the state.[36]

Marx emphasizes, however, that the ruling class does not rule by brute force alone. If it did, it would not rule for long. The longevity and stability of the ruling class's dominance is due to a arguably more important factor : it controls the thoughts, the beliefs and ideas—the "consciousness" of the working class.[37] In a class divided society, says Marx, we will always see "ideology" operating for the benefit of the dominant class and to the detriment of the subservient class.

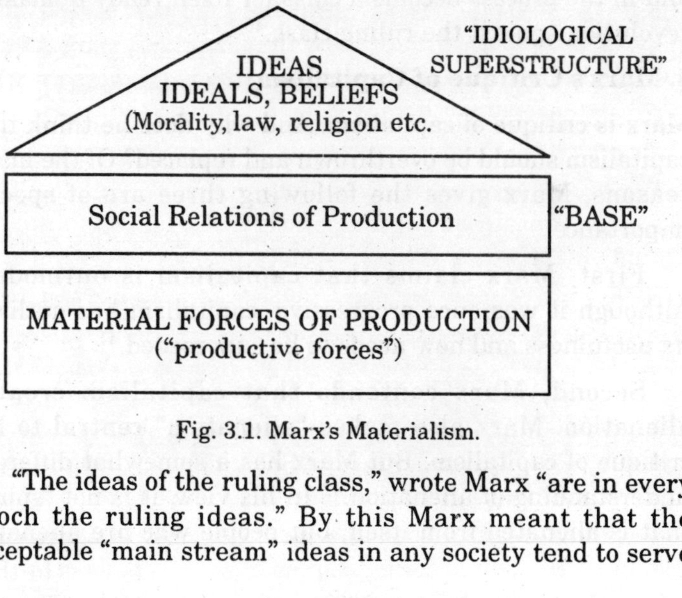

Fig. 3.1. Marx's Materialism.

"The ideas of the ruling class," wrote Marx "are in every epoch the ruling ideas." By this Marx meant that the acceptable "main stream" ideas in any society tend to serve the interests of the ruling class. Individual members of the ruling class may have their differences personal, political and so on—but as a class they share an overriding interest in maintaining the social and economic dominance of their class.[38] In order to do this they must be able to portray their dominance as normal, natural and perhaps even necessary. So, in the ancient Greek society, for example, Aristotle and others said that some people are "slave by nature"—that is, naturally fitted for no other role than that of slave or servant.

Marx called religion "the opiate of the people," because it dulls their minds and makes them uncritical of the wretched conditions in which they live. People living in capitalist society are also taught that it is "human nature" to be self-interested, acquisite and competitive.[39] In all these ways, Marx maintained, the working class is kept from forming a true picture of its red situation. It mistakenly takes the ideas of the ruling class as its own. The working class suffers, in short, from false consciousness. To see how the working class might overcome its false consciousness, and in the process become a class for itself ready to make a revolution against the ruling class.[40]

3. Marx's Critique of Capitalism

Marx is critique of capitalism. And why does he think that capitalism should be overthrown and replaced? Of the many reasons, Marx gives the following three are of special importance.

First, Marx claims that capitalism is outmoded. Although it was once progressive, capitalism has outlived its usefulness and now needs to be superseded.[41]

Second, Marx contends that capitalism creates alienation. Marx also makes "alienation" central to his critique of capitalism. But Marx has a somewhat different understanding of alienation.[42] In his view, it is not "spirit" that is alienated from itself, but people who are alienated from their work and from each other. The sense of alienation felt by the working class will eventually help to bring the downfall of capitalism and the coming of communism.

Under capitalism, Marx maintains, workers are alienated in four distinct but related ways. 1. Because they are forced to sell their labour and do not own what they produce, they are alienated from the product of their labour. 2. Because the capitalist system of mass production kills the creative spirit, workers cannot find satisfaction in their labour and are therefore alienated from the activity of production itself. The worker becomes "an appendage of the machine."[43] 3. Workers are alienated from their distinctively and uniquely human potentials or "powers"—particularly the power to create and enjoy beauty—which are dulled or remain undeveloped in capitalist society. 4. Capitalism alienates workers from each other, in as much as it makes them complete with one another for jobs and wages.

Third, Marx maintains that capitalism is self-subverting.

Marx contends that capitalism has create conditions and unleashed forces that will one day destroy it. In particular, capitalism has created its own "grave diggers" by creating a class—the working class—with interests implacably opposed to its own a class with everything to gain and nothing to lose by revolting against the ruling capitalists. And yet, ironically, it is the capitalist class who are responsible for their own downfall.[44] The working class revolt against the capitalist class. The capitalism is overthrown, abolished and society radically transformed. Marx said the labour class is a "universal class" because in serving its interests, it serves the interests of all humanity. For Marx, then, true freedom from exploitation and alienation, the freedom to develop one's human powers to their fullest—can flourish only in a classless society.[45] It is just this kind of society that workers have an interest in bringing about.

The Revolutionary Sequence

Marx predicted that proletarian revolution, though eventually worldwide, would begin in the more advanced capitalist countries and proceed in a fairly definite order. The stages in the revolutionary sequence can be briefly outlined in the following way.

1. Economic Crises

Capitalism, as Marx was by no means the first to observe, is plagued by periodic economic downturns—recessions and depressions. "Bourgeois" economists call these "fluctuations" in "the business cycle" that will, in time, correct themselves. Marx, on contrast, believed that these crises were due to the "anarchy of production," that characterizes capitalist society. The more mature or advanced a capitalist society becomes, the more frequent and severe these crises will be—and the less likely they are to correct themselves.[46]

2. Immiseration of the Proletariat

The capitalists, being wealthier, are better able to weather these crises than are the workers. Recessions and depressions deprive workers of their jobs, their income, and finally their food and shelter. Unable through no fault of their own to find work, some resort to begging, others to petty thievery for which they risk imprisonment or even death, and still others die of starvation. However, miserable their lot as workers, they become even more miserable when they lose their jobs. This process, the immiseration of the proletariat, is inescapable in capitalist society according to Marx.[47]

3. Revolutionary Class Consciousness

The workers in their misery begin to realize that the fault lies not with them but with the system—a system beset by "contradictions" too glaring to pass unnoticed. They are willing to work, but there are not enough jobs to go around. The bourgeois "coupon clippers" who do not work are nevertheless comfortable and affluent. Their, children, well fed and warmly clothed, go to school the worker's children—malnourished, hungry, and ill clad-beg in the streets and dig through garbage for scraps of food.[48] Seeing these contradictions leads workers to reflect critically on the causes of their misery. In this process, moreover, Marx's theory intervenes to make a contribution of its own, it supplies an explanation of how things came to be this way. It also proposes a solution; the overthrow of the ruling bourgeoisie. Because Marx believed that the workers would sooner or later arrive at this conclusion on their own he saw himself as merely a "midwife" reducing the "births pangs" by hastening the revolutionary process along the most direct and least painful course.[49]

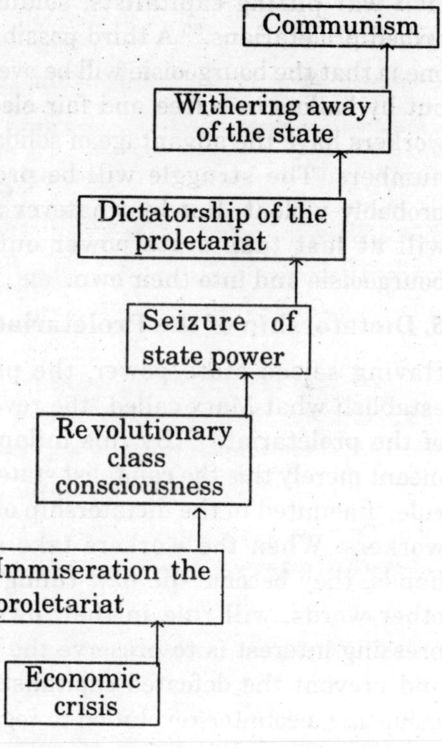

Fig. 3.2. Marx's view of the revolutionary sequence.

4. Seizure of State Power

Marx predicted that "objective" economic conditions (the economic crises resulting in the immiseration of the proletariat) and "subjective" conditions (revolutionary class consciousness) would bine to form a politically explosive mixture. Beginning with the apparently unrelated, small spontaneous strikes, boycotts, demonstrations, and riot, the revolutionary movement quickly coalesces into a more militant, organized, and unified force for the overthrow of the ruling class. Marx believed that this could come about in a number of ways. One possibility is that a nationwide "general strike" will cripple the economy and bankrupt the capitalists almost overnight. Another possibility is a bloody civil war pitting capitalists, soldiers and police against armed proletarians.[50] A third possibility, albeit an unlikely one is that the bourgeoisie will be overthrown not by bullets, but by ballots in a free and fair election. In any case, the workers have the advantage of solidarity and sheer force of numbers. The struggle will be protracted, difficult and probably violent. But by whatever means, the proletariat will at last take state power out of the hands of the bourgeoisie and into their own.

5. Dictatorship of the Proletariat

Having seized state power, the proletariat proceeds to establish what Marx called "the revolutionary dictatorship of the proletariat."[51] By this inflammatory phrase, Marx meant merely this the capitalist state being a system of class rule, amounted to the dictatorship of the capitalist over the workers. When the workers take state power into their hands, they become the new ruling class. The workers, in other words, will rule in their own interest. Their most pressing interest is to preserve the gains of the revolution and prevent the defeated capitalists from regrouping and mounting a counter-revolution to regain power. The working class must, accordingly, use the apparatus of the state—the schools, courts, prisons and police—in as "dictatorial" a manner as necessary to prevent this possibility. Marx expects the victorious workers to be democratic and open in their dealing with each other. Theirs is to be a dictatorship of and by, not over, the proletariat.[52]

6. Withering Away of the State

Under socialism, according to Marx, the rule should be : "from each according to his ability, to each according to his labour". But the abiding interest of the proletariat, the "universal class", is in abolishing classes and class distinctions. This will begin to happen once the workers take control of the workplace and transform the conditions of labour, ending exploitation and alienation. As the capitalist die out, or see the errors of their ways, the need for coercion will gradually fade. Marx expects, then, that "the dictatorship of the proletariat" will lose its reason for existing and simply "wither away."[53]

7. Communism

Marx said remarkably little about the specific features of a future communist society. The shape of any future society, Marx thought, could only be decided by the people who would inhabit it. Marx thought, could only be decided by the people who would inhabit it. Even so, Marx did hint at several features that he thought such a society will have. For one, it will be open and democratic, with all citizens taking an active part in governing it. For another, the major means of production—mills, mines, factories, and so on will be publicly owned. Economic production will be planned and orderly. And distribution of goods and services will be based not on privilege or wealth, but on ability and need. Under communism, then, the rule will be : "From each according to his ability, to each according to his need." People living in a communist society will at last be truly free. Having overcome the obstacles of exploitation, alienation, and ideological illusions, that is, they will be free to develop their many sided personalities. Marx thus envisioned a future society in which every human being, not just a fortunate few, will be free to become well rounded Renaissance men and women.

Marx died in 1883—too early to witness attempts to put his ideas into political practice. Others, however, calling themselves Marxists and claiming to speak in his name, were soon busy interpreting, reinterpreting and adapting his ideas in ways that would almost certainly have astonished, and in some cases appalled, Karl Marx. Whether Marx would have liked it or not, he gave rise to Marxism.

CONCLUSION

Socialism as an Ideology

Like Liberalism and conservatism, socialism comes in so many varieties that it sometimes seems to be not one, but many different ideologies. Socialists do share certain core assumptions or beliefs, however, just as liberals and conservatives do. To see what these are, we must note how socialism performs the four functions that all political ideologies perform.

1. Explanation

To begin with, how do socialists try to explain social conditions? In general, they explain them interms of economic and class relations. Rather than appeal to be choices of individuals, as liberals typically do, socialists are inclined to say that individuals are always caught up in social relations that shape and structure the choices available to them. Individuals may make choices, but they cannot choose to do just anything they wish. As Marx put it, "Men make their own history, but they do not make it just as they please." Some will have more to choose from others. In particular, capitalists will have more options than workers, and the choices that capitalists make will sharply limit the choices available to the workers. A capitalist faced with declining profits can decide to expand or reinvest in his or her business, for instance, or move it to a different region or country, or simply sell or close it. Within the limits of his or her resources, the capitalist can do as he or she sees fit. But the worker can usually do nothing more than react to the choice the capitalist makes. And when the capitalist decides to close the business, the worker has little choice but to look elsewhere for work.[54]

2. Evaluation

This carries over to the second function of ideologies, that of evaluating social conditions. In this case the key factor is the sharpness of class divisions in a society. If one class of people clearly has firm control of the wealth, so that it is able to limit sharply the choices open to the working class, then conditions are, from the socialist point of view, exploitative and unjust. If class division are slight, or if there are no apparent classes at all, then conditions will be much better. But this can only happen, socialist say, if control of the major means of production is somehow shared by all members of the society.[55]

3. Orientation

As regards orientation, socialists tell people that they should think of themselves mainly in terms of their position in the class structure. Some socialists have taken this to the extreme of saying that class differences are the only differences that matter. When Marx said that the workers have no fatherland, for instance, he seemed to say that nationality or citizenship should play no real role in one's identity. Not race or religion or nationality, but only class position really makes a difference in the world.[56]

According to socialists, class consciousness is a necessary step on the path to a classless society. Before a capitalist can see the error of his or her ways, the capitalist must first understand that he or she is a member of the class that exploits and oppresses the workers. Only then is there any chance that the capitalist will surrender control of wealth and resources to their rightful owner—society at large. More importantly, it is only when the workers see that they form a large and oppressed class that they will be able to take action to free themselves. If they fail to develop this awareness of their social position, they will have no more chance of liberating themselves than the slave who thinks that his or her slavery is altogether natural and proper.[57]

4. Programme

For most socialist then, orientation is necessary to the programmatic function of their ideology. The socialist goal is simple : to bring about a society that is as nearly classless as possible. Exactly how they propose to do this will vary from one time and place to another, of course. Some look for an almost spontaneous revolution, as we have seen, while others believe a single highly disciplines party must lead the way, some rely on persuasion and the force of example, while others favour violent revolution and the force of arms. But in all cases they maintain the steps must be taken to promote equality and co-operation among all members of society in order to give everyone greater control over his or her own life.[58]

Socialism and the Democratic Ideal

In its pursuit of equality, socialism is an ideology committed to democracy in one or another sense of that contested term. As most socialists will quickly admit, leaders like stalin have been more interested in acquiring personal power than in promoting democracy, but these leaders, they say, were not true socialists. True socialism requires government of by, and for the people. It aims to give everyone an equal voice in the decisions that affect his or her life in direct and important ways. But this can only happen, socialists say, if no one person or class controls most of the wealth and resources—and thus most of the power within a society.[59] Wealth and resources must be shared evenly and owned and controlled for the benefit of the whole society if true democracy is ever to take shape. Otherwise, they insist, we shall have nothing but government of the wealthy, by the wealthy, and for the wealthy.[60]

REFERENCES

1. Leszek Kolakowski, Main Currents of Marxism, Vol. II, The Golden Age (Oxford : Clarendon Press, 1978).
2. For one history of socialism among many, See George Lichtheim, A Short History of Socialism (New York : Praeger, 1970).
3. Plato, The Republic (Books III and IV, 412 B-421 C).
4. Thomas More, Utopia, ed., J. Churlton Collins (Oxford : Clarendon Press, 1904), pp. 43–44.
5. *Ibid.,* p. 68.
6. Gerrard Winstanley, A New Years Gift for the Parliament and Armie (1650).
7. Saint Simon, Social Organization, The Sciences of Man and Order Writings, ed., Felix Markham (New York : Harper Torchbooks, 1964).
8. Auguste Comte, Auguste Comte and Positivism : Selection from His Writings, ed., Felix Markham (New York : Harper Torchbooks, 1964), pp. 88.
9. See Frank E. Manuel, The Prophets of Paris (Cambridge, M.A. Harvard University Press, 1962).
10. Robert Owen, A New View of Society and Other Writings, ed., G.D.H. Cole (London : E.P. Dent, 1927), for an excerpt, see Ball and Dagger, Ideals and Ideologies, Selection 33.
11. David McLellan, Marx, His Life and Thought (London Macmillan, 1973).
12. G.W.F. Hegel, Phenomenology of Mind, trans : (New York : Harper and Row, 1967), 228–240.
13. Karl Marx, Capital (New York : International Publishers, 1967), Vol. I, “Afterword to the Second German Edition”, p. 20.
14. Marx and Engels, Basic Writings of Politics and Philosophy (Garden City, NY : Doubleday Anchor, 1959), p., 7, also in Ideals and Ideologies, Selection 34.
15. All quotations in this paragraph are from Marx and Engels, The German Ideology, Part I, (New York : International Publishers, 1947).

16. Manifesto, p. 9.
17. German Ideology, p. 39, Manifesto, p. 26.
18. Manifesto, p. 9.
19. *Ibid.,* pp. 9–10.
20. *Ibid.,* p. 12.
21. *Ibid.,* p. 10.
22. *Ibid.,* p. 14.
23. *Ibid.,* p. 22.
24. German Ideology, p. 14.
25. Berlin Isaiah, Karl Marx, His Life and Environment, 4th ed., Oxford University Press, 1978.
26. Carver, Terrell, Marx's Social Theory, Oxford : Oxford University Press, 1982.
27. Cohen, G.A., Karl Marx's Theory of History (Princeton University Press, 1978).
28. Gilbert Alan, Marx's Politics : Communists and Citizens, New Burns Wick, NJ : Princeton University Press, 1978.
29. Kolakowski, Leszek, Main Currents of Marxism, 3 Vols., trans. P.S. Falla, Oxford : Clarendon Press, 1978.
30. McLellan, David, Karl Marx, His Life and Thought, London : Macmillan, 1973.
31. Wilson, Edmund, To the Finland Station, New York : Doubleday Anchor, 1953.
32. Quoted in David McLellan, Karl Marx, His Life and Work (London Macmillan 1973), p. 443.
33. Marx, "Theses on Feuerbach" in Selected Works, p. 28.
34. Peter Gay, The Dilemma of Democratic Socialism, 2nd ed., (New York : Collier Books, 1962).
35. Bernstein, Evolutionary Socialism, p. 106.
36. *Ibid.,* p. 210, also in Ideals and Ideologies, Selection 36.
37. *Ibid.,* p. 202.
38. Bernstein, Evolutionary Socialism, p. 211.
39. *Ibid.,* p. 219.

40. See Gary P. Steenson, 1854-1938 : Marxism in the Classical Years (Pittsburgh : University of Pittsburgh Press, 1978), esp., pp. 116-131 and 186.
41. Quoted in Kolakowski, Main Currents of Marxism, Vol. II, p. 386.
42. Roy A. Medvedev, Let History Judge (New York : Viking Press, 1973).
43. Medvedev, Let History Judge, p. 510.
44. See Paul Thomas, Karl Marx and the Anarchists (London : Routledge and Kegan Paul, 1980).
45. William Godwin, An Enquiry Concerning Political Justice (London : Duckworth, 1984).
46. Peter Kropotkin, Mutual aid (London : Heinemann, 1902).
47. Emma Goldman, Anarchism and other Essays (New York : Mother Earth Association, 1910), p. 58 and p. 68, also in Ideals and Ideologies, Selection 41.
48. See Michael Harrington, Socialism : Past, Present and Future (New York : Penguin Books, USA, 1990).
49. Crick, Bernard, Socialism, University of Minnesota Press, 1987.
50. Gay, Peter, *op. cit.*, pp. 67-70.
51. Miller David, *op. cit.*, pp. 80-85.
52. Lichtheim, George, A Short History of Socialism, New York : Praeger, 1970, pp. 70-75.
53. *Ibid., op. cit.*, pp. 75-80.
54. *Ibid., op. cit.*, pp. 80-85.
55. *Ibid., op. cit.*, pp. 90-100.
56. *Ibid., op. cit.*, pp. 105-106.
57. *Ibid., op. cit.*, pp. 110-115.
58. *Ibid., op. cit.*, pp. 120-125.
59. *Ibid., op. cit.*, pp. 130-135.
60. *Ibid., op. cit.*, pp. 145-150.

4

DEMOCRATIC SOCIALISM

Introduction

As the name implies, democratic socialism is a synthesis of or half-way house between democracy and socialism. It is very difficult to give a clear idea of what democratic socialism really means. Democratic socialism is an evolutionary socialism, it is as a concept and an ideology. It is the product of the twentieth century and a theory of recent origin.

Origin

The origin of the democratic socialism can be traced back to U.K., the mother of parliamentary institutions which was primarily responsible for bringing out a compromise between democracy (political aspect) and socialism (social aspect).[1] In other words, democratic socialism, as a political concept originated in England where G.D.H. Cole, Sidney, Webbs, Tawney, Robert Owen, H.J. Laski and many others contributed to its growth. Prof. Durbin's greater work "the politics of democratic socialism", has been regarded as the 'Bible' for democratic socialism, a model and guide for all the democratic countries.[2] The Labour Party in U.K. was also responsible for sowing the seeds of democratic socialism. The labour party in England has expressed its faith in democratic socialism. Prof. Harold J. Laski was a democratic socialist, who openly condemned the violent path of socialism, as he believed firmly in the principles of liberty and equality as the two pillars of a true democracy. The spirit of democratic socialism is also true in U.S.A. though, it is capitalist in terms of its economy but the U.S.A. never tolerates the entry of Marxism or communism.[3]

The writings and the great works of great writers like Robert Owen, Durbin, G.D.H. Cole, Prof. Laski etc. have exerted the tremendous impact and influence on the most of the European countries like U.K., Sweden as they have wedded themselves to the path of democratic socialism. But countries like Poland, Russia, Yugoslavia, China etc. have embraced and experimented with communism.[4]

India's Experiment with Democratic Socialism

India's experiment with democratic socialism started with Pandit Jawaharlal Nehru, who is considered to be the architect of modern India. As a national leader in the nationalist movement for freedom, he fought for national Independence.[5] After independence, as the first Prime Minister of India, he struggled, dedicated and devoted to the national cause of economic and social development. Though, Nehru was aristocrat by birth but he was a democrat by training. He was a great democrat, a great socialist, and a great secularist with scientific bent of mind, with pragmatic and practical approach to the problems.[6]

Now the Question is : What made Nehru to adopt democratic socialism only? Though, Nehru had studied and admired different bands of socialism especially Marxism, but he rejected it on the ground that it believed in violent, radical and revolutionary means and methods to achieve the end, because Nehru was the close disciple of Mahatma Gandhi, who believed in non-violence, peace and truth. Secondly, according to Nehru, the poverty and backwardness of India was due to the British policy of exploitation, colonialism and imperialism. So, he felt and came to a firm conclusion that the only answer and the way to put an end to mass poverty, misery and backwardness of India was to adopt democratic socialism so as to establish a 'socialist society' or welfare state—which was to serve as an answer to all the evils of capitalism, colonialism and imperialism etc.[7]

Nehru's Commitment to socialist ideas was expressed by him at Lahore session of Indian National Congress as early as in lazy. He said "I must frankly confess that I am a socialist and a Republican and no believer in kings and princes. We must realise that the philosophy of socialism has gradually permeated the entire structure of society the world over and almost the only points in dispute are the peace and methods of advance to its full realisation. India will have to go that way too, if she seeks to end her poverty, and inequality.[8]

Under the able and dynamic leadership of Pandit Nehru, after Independence, The Indian National Congress as its sessions adopted number of resolutions for building or establishing socialist pattern of society. According to Nehru, "Socialism is the outcome of democracy and political democracy has no meaning unless it embraces economic democracy.[9]

In December 1954, in a speech to Lok Sabha Nehru explained the concept as "the pattern of society that we look forward to is a socialist pattern of society which is classless and casteless."[10] So, at the Avadi session, the goal of socialistic pattern of society was officially accepted again at 68 the session of the Indian National Congress at Bhubaneshwer in 1964 decided to follow the path of democratic socialism for bringing about welfare state. At Bhubaneshwar Nehru said—"We shall be able to establish a socialist society without class conflict." Thus, Nehru contributed a lot towards establishing a state for the economic and social development of India. Later the path of Nehru was followed by stalwarts like Ashok Mehta, Jayaprakash Narayan and others."

Nehru thought interms of mixing socialism with democracy. Democracy means removal of inequality, disparities, differences and distinctions. In his theory of economic democracy, Nehru said, the good things of life must be available to more and more people and gross inequalities must be removed. Socialism appealed to him "as a philosophy of life." Socialism is the only key to the solution of the India's and the world problems. He stated that he was drawn towards socialism from his younger days. A classless society according to him should be our ultimate goal *i.e.,* equality of opportunity and economic justice. Everything that comes in the way will have to be removed gently if possible, forcibly if necessary.[12]

Jawaharlal Nehru evolved his own ideas about socialism and he tried to give them a practical shape.[13] He developed a deep faith in the ultimate success of socialism as a remedy of human ills. He said there is no other way of ending poverty, unemployment, degradation and the subjection of the people except through socialism. Any method which delivers the good could be used and the method need not necessarily to be an extreme method belonging to either of these two rival ideologies—capitalism and socialism, but could be something in between". He thus, seemed to be in favour of a "Mixed Economy".[14]

Jawaharlal Nehru proceeded to work for a democratic socialist state. Hasty action seemed to him full of risks and dangers. Working on his socialist ideas and plans, he attached great importance to the public sector as against the private sector. If the state wants to take the property, every step should be taken to ensure the individuals receiving fair and equitable compensation.[15]

Nehru came to believe that the employer and the worker relationship could be based more on judicious principles in modern times. The conflict could be resolved through mutual understanding and conciliation. He was in favour of trade unions and of labourer's right to strike. But what worried him was the wastage involved in strikes and lock-outs. What he wanted, therefore, was that their should be faith in mutual agreement or if that was not possible, there should be faith in some third party in the form of conciliator, arbitrator or tribunal.[16]

He pointed out rightly that all the great things in this world had not been achieved or done through acquisitiveness, but by the reverse of it. Great inventors, scientists, writers, academicians, musicians and engineers proposed and made the world advance because of other urges.[17] Thus, he advocated a broader consideration of social relations and social interests as the means towards social and economic equality. And it was through, peace and not through conflict that he proceeded and worked to bring about socialism in India.

Jawaharlal thought that both socialism and democracy meant removal of disparities or establishment of social and economic equality in society. Therefore, socialism should follow democratic lines and keep itself away from any kind of authoritarianism. He felt that it was necessary for any community to work for the establishment of social and economic justice.[18] Material well being of the people could also be brought about through fascist means, but there would be no chance in a fascist regime for an individual to grow and think freely. His voice would be suppressed for the sake of uniformity.

Socialism Under Mrs. Indira Gandhi

Pandit Jawaharlal Nehru served India for more than 17 years as the great statesmen, great leader, great democrat and a great socialist being the first prime minister of free India. The type of socialism as adopted and advocated by Nehru has been followed and continued by Mrs. Indira Gandhi. When Mrs. Indira Gandhi came to power after the death of Lal Bahadur Shastri, she started to launch number of economic programmes under the orbit of the Indian National Congress to achieve social and economic justice for all the people of India.[19] So in 1967, the Congress Party accepted 10 Point Economic Programme as the end towards establishing Socialist Democratic Society. Some of the important points were :

1. Social control of banking institutions, but this was violated as 14 banks were nationalised.
2. Nationalisation of General Insurance.
3. Commodity wise progress in state trading in imports and exports.
4. Expansion of Cooperatives.
5. State trading in food grains.
6. Regulated removal of monopolies by Act.
7. Minimum needs to the community.
8. Unearned increments in urban land revenues.
9. Rural work programme and land reform.
10. Abolition of privy purses.

Again in 1975 July 1 under the leadership of Mrs. Indira Gandhi 20 point programme was adopted towards the goal of achieving economic and social justice by the Congress Party. The programme included the following some of the important points :

1. Strict economy in government expenditure.
2. Implementation of agricultural land ceilings.
3. Abolition of bonded labour.
4. New schemes for workers association in industry.
5. Books and stationary at controlled rates etc.

Emergency was proclaimed or declared by president of India Mr. Fakruddin Ali Ahmed on June 26, 1975, for the speedy implementation of 20 point programme. All the states were required to extend their fullest cooperation for the speedy implementation of the programme. So, a beginning was made towards the goal of socialism, but unfortunately due to the excesses of emergency, there was a greater reaction against the Mrs. Gandhi's government and as such electrons were held and Mrs. Gandhi was defeated and Janata Party came to power in 1977. So the implementation of 20 point programme got weakened.[20]

Unique Goals and Features of Indian Brand of Democratic Socialism

The type of socialism that India has adopted as a result of initiative of Mr. Pandit Nehru is some what 'unique' in the sense, it is a sort of economic creed to serve the interests of the Indians. Some of the unique goals and features of Indian brand of socialism are said to be as follows :

1. Socialism stands for putting an end to poverty, unemployment, economic inequality and social degradation.
2. In stands for introducing revolutionary changes in political and social structure of the country.
3. It stands for eliminating undesirable effects of property system.
4. It stands for replacing the motive for personal profit by the ideal of co-operative service.
5. Democracy and socialism should go hand in hand.
6. Power has to be secured through amicable, peaceful and democratic means (power through ballot but not through bullet).
7. Social change has to be brought about through legislation but not through revolutions.
8. 'Mixed Economy' is a peculiar contribution of India in which socialist state reins number of industries and also allows the private enterprises to flourish in several areas of economy. It means encouraging both public and private sectors.

9. Democratic socialism is an economic creed to be achieved through planning. Planning is the means or the basis for achieving the goals of democratic socialism. That is why the second five year plan had the basic goal of establishing a 'socialist pattern of society' by increasing agricultural and industrial production, raising standard of living of the people, removing or reducing the wide gap between the rich and the poor and ensuring economic equality. It was again Pandit Nehru, who was responsible for launching economic planning in India for economic development, so as to achieve the goals of social and economic justic.[21]

Dilemmas of Democratic Socialism in India

Indian brand of socialism has run into many problems, troubles and pitfalls. It has to been successful to the expectations of the Indians. Why it has not been successful? For this many reasons can be given and many factors are responsible. It has been receiving criticisms and reactions from great scholars and parliamentarians like J.B. Kriplani.

In February 1970, in an Article entitled "What sort of socialism", J.B. Kriplani has made some critical observations on Indian brand of socialism as :

1. Socialism in India consists of politicians and party bosses, their dominance and dictatorship.
2. Leaders are narrow-minded, communal and caste oriented.
3. Educational institutions and facilities are meant only for the children's of politicians and rich people.
4. Equality is unknown to the villagers.
5. Labour class is completely ignored or neglected.
6. Press and Radio are devoted completely for the politicians and men in power.

Despite such criticisms, there are other reasons for which we can say that socialism in India has not been successful. Those reasons can be summed up as follows.

1. Party Politics

India has been completely dominated by party politics. Party politics has become more important than economic development. In the western countries, economic development is more important than politics. The game of politics in India is played only for the sake of politics. Politics is not characterised by stability due to splits in political parties.[22] Different political parties have their own splits as Congress party has Congress (I), National Congress Party, Janata Party of Chandra Shekhar, Biju Janata Dal of Patnayak, BJP of Atal Behari Vajpayee, CPI, CPM, PSP, DMK, AIADMK, RJD, Jana Shakti Samata Party etc. These multi party system has created a confusion in the minds of the voters. No party has established its credibility in the voters. It has become very difficult to say, which party stands for what? All political parties have become too opportunistic just to play the game of politics, to get power and to misuse power. All parties are engaged in how to get power, how to retain power and how to expand power. The 'Ideals' like socialism, democratic socialism, secularism, have liberty, equality, or eternity and justice have been used as the means of propaganda by the political parties to win the elections. So, the ideals and ideologies have lost their meaning, spirit[23] and importance.

Those who contest or fight or stand elections spend money in terms of lakhs or crores together, just to purchase the votes by making false promises, by fooling and misguiding the voters. Thus, it is clear that the game of politics is played through the means of money, muscle and mafia power. The slogans, ideologies statements at the time of elections are used as the means to win the elections. If this is so, how is it possible to make socialism meaningful, fruitful colourful and successful.[24]

2. Failure of Planning

It is said that "Indian are good planners, but bad doers".[25] It is true that planning is the means to achieve the goals of democratic socialism. But as we notice today, there is no timely implementation of the plans. There is a wide gap or gulf between planning and its implementation process. The plans have not been able to reach their targets. As such, neither agricultural nor industrial production has increased so as to raise the standard of living of the people to increase the national income or to build a socialistic pattern of society. The failure of planning has been caused on account of natural calamities or epidemics like, floods, famine, earthquake and also on account of lack of financial resources. The government has been forced to resort to 'deficit' financing as a result of this, people are forced to pay heavy taxes.[26]

3. Evils of Bureaucracy

The Government administration in India has been proved too weak and inefficient as it cares more for the rules, regulations and formalities without carrying for the real needs aspirations and problems of the citizens. Corruption has become too routine in governmental administration. There is no co-ordination between the higher and lower levels of bureaucracy. Friction is found everywhere. Corruption cannot be eradicated or eliminated so easily either by law or by any ordinance of the government. Both citizens and the government are equally held responsible for the evil of corruption,[27] and corruption has became the order of the day or a fashion.

We talk of neat, clean, and efficient administration, but in practice, quite reverse is the result. So, the evils like red-tape, nepotism and corruption etc. have become the hurdles or bickerings in the way of achieving of goals of socialism.

4. Agitations

Last but not the least, we see in each and every corner of the country there has been discontent, disappointment, dissatisfaction and frustration, apathy among the workers, teacher, government servants, students, farmers, labourers, and among the common people. More than 40% of the Indian people are living below poverty line. They are not in a position to get their basic minimums–like food, clothing and shelter (रोटी, कपड़ा और मकान). Hence, farmers agitations or strikes for fair price for their products, students agitations for employment, workers agitations for their good conditions of work, labourers agitations for higher wages, teachers and government servants agitations for higher salary, the people's agitations due to inflationary tendencies.[28]

In such are the Indian conditions and problems, the goal of socialism cannot be achieved or attained. Democratic socialism in India is in a dilemma facing such serious and severe problems and challenges. So, the problem ends with no conclusion.

REFERENCES

1. Engels, Socialism, Utopian and Scientific, in Marx and Engels, Selected Works. Also in Terence Ball and Richard Daggar, eds., Ideals and Ideologies : A Reader, 3rd ed., (New York : Longman, 1999), Selection 35.
2. Eduard Bernstein, Evolutionary Socialism (New York : Schocken Books, 1961), p. 202.
3. Lenin, "Left Wing" Communism–An Infantil Disorder, in Selected Works, p. 535.
4. Quoted in Kolakowski, Main Currents of Marxism, Vol. II, p. 386.
5. Jawaharlal Nehru is rightly regarded as the founder of democratic socialism in India.
6. Nehru was a pragmatic and practical and not dogmatic. His approach to the problems are scientific and empirical.

7. Bernstein, Evolutionary Socialism, p. 106.
8. *Ibid.*, p. 210, also in Ideals and Ideologies, Selection 36.
9. Nehru quoted political democracy and economic democracy are the two parts of the same coin.
10. Medredev, Let History Judge, p. 510.
11. After Nehru, Galaxy of Indian Social and Political Reformers followed democratic socialism.
12. Machiavelli quoted in his book 'prince' there are two methods of fighting. 1. Fight by law, 2. Fight by force. This statement is aptly applied here.
13. See Michael Harrington, Socialism : Past and Future (New York : Penguin Books, U.S.A., 1990).
14. "Mixed Economy" means encouraging both public and private sectors.
15. William Godwin, An Enquiry Concerning Political Justice ed. (London : Duckworth, 1984). That is why it is said that haste is waste, hurry leads to worry.
16. Conciliation is one of the peaceful or amicable means or methods of settling the disputes.
17. Quoted in Bruce Mazlish, The Revolutionary Ascetic (New York : Basic Books, 1976), p. 140. Curiority is the mother of invention.
18. Skinner, Quentin, The Foundations of Modern Political Thought, 2 Vols., Cambridge : Cambridge University Press, 1978.
19. Pateman, Carole, Participation and Democratic Theory, Cambridge University Press, 1997.
20. Any kind of National Emergency Spoils the image of the Nation.
21. Plato's Republic, pp. 45–50.
22. Now-a-days, Indian Politics is characterised by instability.
23. Now-a-days Politician at the time of elections use propaganda and mass media as a means to misguide the people.
24. Now-a-days at the time of Elections 3 M's plays a very important role *i.e.,* Money power, Muscle power and Mafia power.

25. This proverb or idea is drawn from the Prof. Krishna Aiyer's Book 'Public Administration', pp. 45–50.
26. Macpherson, C.B., "The Life and Times of Liberal Democracy".
27. Corruption is compared to a cancer disease. It paralyses every organ of the body.
28. Held, David, Models of Democracy, Standford, PCA : Standford University Press, 1986.

In India, today we found unrest everywhere. Murder, killing, kidnapping are the order of the day.

5

ENVIRONMENTALISM

Introduction

The idea of that the relationship between human-beings and the natural world is politically important is of relatively recent origin. Until the 1960s, nature was regarded by most political thinkers as nothing more than an 'economic resource' available for human beings to exploit, more or less efficiently.[1] The earth's human population has continued of expand 5.3 billion people are alive today and it is estimated that this will grow to 8.5 billion by the year 2025. At the same time, human beings in all parts of the world, but particularly in the industrialised West, have demanded higher standards of living and greater affluence, which can only be achieved by utilising greater quantities of the earth's resources.[2]

As a concern about environmental issues has grown, a distinctive set of political ideas and values has emerged which openly challenge established ideologies of left, right and centre.[3] As yet, this new ideology lacks a single agreed title. However, as a result of the development T.H. Green (German), Green ideas, the term has been linked to the specific ideas and policies of such parties, rather than principles of the larger environmental movement. 'Ecology' is commonly used to indicate the interrelatedness of natural life, a fundamental principle of environmental thought. The term 'ecology' was coined by Ernst Haeckel in 1858, and it refer to a branch of biology which studies the relationship amongst living organisms and their environment.[4] All environmental thinkers respect the principles of ecology.

'Environmentalism' is a broad term which has been used since the 1950s to refer to a range of ideas and theories. In other words, environmentalism covers a brand range of theories, scientific, religious, economic and political, rather than a particular set of policies, such as those endorsed by the contemporary green movement.[5] However, environmentalism constitutes a distinctive and coherent political ideology and embody the relationship between human kind and nature. However, to a large extent, environmentalism was, and still remains, a reaction against the process of industrialisation.[6]

But the growth of environmentalism in the late twentieth century has been provoked by the relentless progress of industralisation and urbanisation. Environmental concern has been more acute and radical because of the fear that economic growth threatens to endanger both the survival of the human race and the very planet it lives upon.[7]

Environmental politics has clearly drawn attention to issues like pollution, conservatism, 'acid rain', the 'green house effect' and global warming. He environmental movement has addressed a far broader range of issues.[8] The Green in Germany, for instance, have campained on the role of women, defence and disarmament, the welfare state and unemployment, and the need for a re-examination of Germany's Nazi past, as well as on narrower environmental issues. More significantly, environmentalists have developed a radically new set of concepts and values with which to understand and explain the world. Environmentalism has developed into a distinctive ideology which stands apart from traditional political creeds.[9] It starts with the examination of the relationship between humankind and nature.

2. Back to Nature

Environmentalists has criticised the most basic assumption upon which conventional political thought is based. John Cocke said human beings have become the masters and possessors of nature. Environmentalists, warn, tragically unbalanced the relationship between humankind and nature. Environmentalism represents a new style of politics. Human kind no longer occupies centre state, but is regarded as an inseparable part of nature.[10] Human beings are therefore, required to practise humility, moderation and gentleness, and to give up the misguided dream that science and technology can solve all their problems.

The central principle of all forms of environmentalism is ecology. Ecology is the study of plants and animals in relationship to each other and their natural environment. Ecology literally means the study of organisms 'at home' or 'in their habitats' and developed as a distinct branch of biology in the early twentieth century. But ecosystems composed of both living and non-living elements.[11] A simple example of an ecosystem world be a field, forest, pond or even puddle. In a pond, for instance, the sediment lying at the bottom contains nutrients which support various kinds of plant life. These plants provide oxygen and food which sustain the fish and insects living in the pond. All ecosystems tend towards a state of harmony or balance through a system of self-regulation. Food and other resources are recycled and the population size of animals, insects and plants adjust naturally to the available food supply. However, such ecosystems are not 'closed' or entirely self-sustaining each interacts with the other ecosystems.[12]

A lake may itself constitute an ecosystem, but it also needs to be fed with fresh water from tributaries and receive warmth and energy from the sun. The lake, in turn, provides water and food for species living along its shores, including human communities. The natural world is therefore, made up of a complex web of ecosystems, the largest of which is the global ecosystem, commonly called the 'ecosphere' or 'biosphere'.[13]

But the problems is the world's population has increased five-fold, with currently 220,000 babies born each day, 150 every minute. The earth has become over-burdened with an exploding human population, which has given little thought to how its new members are going to be fed, clothed or housed. Finite and irreplaceable fuel resources, such as coal, oil, and natural gas are being used up with reckless abandon.[14]

Ecology provides a radically different vision of nature and the place of human beings within it. Some environmentalists, regard ecology as the key to human survival and well being.[15] Ecology requires, in effect a new conception of human nature. Human beings are not the masters of their own destiny, but they are rather, inescapably part of the nature. Humankind is merely one organism within a complex biosphere.[16]

In searching for this new paradigm, environmental thinkers have been attracted to a variety of ideas and theories, drawn from both modern science and ancient myths and religions. However, the unifying theme amongst these ideas is the notion of holism. Holism is based upon the belief that 'the whole' is more important than its individual parts, indeed it suggests that each part only has a meaning in relation to other parts and ultimately, in relation to 'the whole'.[17]

In medical science, for example, disease has traditionally been understood and treated as a defect of a particular organ or even of specific cells within the body, not an imbalance within the life of the patient as a whole. Attention has therefore been paid to the treatment of physical symptoms while psychological social or environmental factors have tended to be ignored.[18] In the case of heart disease, conventional medicine has made remarkable advances, for instance, in correcting or replacing defective heart valves, transplanting human hearts, and even developing artificial hearts. However, it has often neglected psychological factors like stress, or social and environmental factors such as smoking, diet and pollution which may have caused the condition in the first place. A holistic approach to health therefore tries to treat the 'whole person' understanding injuries or disease as only a physical symptom of what may be a complex range of factors, physical, psychological social and environmental. Such holistic principles have deeply impressed environmental thinkers intent upon discovering new approaches to social, economic and political problems. Indeed, holism implies that the traditional division of human knowledge into separate compartments-science, philosophy, history, politics and so on-is redundant. Economics for example, can no longer be regarded simply as the study of the production and consumption of goods.[19] A holistic approach to economics requires that the environmental cost of production, its spiritual or moral value, and its political consequences, must also be taken into account. Thus, the world now has been abandoned by many scientists.[20]

Primitive religions often drew no distinction between human life and other forms of life, and indeed little distinction between living and non-living objects.[21] All things were alive, stones, rivers, mountains and even the earth itself, often conceived of as 'Mother Earth'. The idea of an Earth Mother has been particularly important for environmentalists trying to articulate a new relationship between human beings and natural world. Environmentalists have usually wished to change policies and attitudes in order to ensure the continued survival of the human species.[22]

The application of ecological or holistic principles to human life and conduct would require a radical, even revolutionary, change. The modern world has witnessed the triumph of technology over nature, as human beings, armed with ever—more impressive scientific knowledge, confidently believed they had the capacity to solve all problems. All parts of the world, even the countryside itself, bear a human imprint. Human beings have tamed, civilised and even replaced nature. Life is increasingly lived in a synthetic environment, one fashioned by technology and human ingenuity.[23]

Environmentalists argue that science and technology have been, at best, a mixed blessing for the human race. There is no doubt that science has unlocked many of the "secrets of nature" but its promise to make human kind the master of its own destiny has proved to be illusory. Orthodox science has sought greater and greater knowledge of the 'world-machine' by examining its component parts. Human beings are blessed with massive 'knowhow' and material wealth, but possess precious little 'knowwhy'.[24]

Environmentalists are agreed the when 'progress' or 'development' is understood in material terms alone it becomes self defeating. Moreover, industrial life has led to alienation and isolation as human beings struggle to live in a manmade environment of concrete and bricks, without the support of caring communities or a sense of rootedness in nature. In underlining our dependence upon natural processes, environmentalism seeks to re-establish balance between humankind and nature, and, in the process, create more rounded and fulfilled human beings. However, this goal requires a new attitude to science and technology.

3. Politics and the Environment

Like nationalism and feminism, environmentalism can be regarded as a cross-cutting ideology. At different times, liberals, socialists, anarchists, conservatives and even fascists have claimed a special sympathy with the environment and environmental ideas have been enlisted in support of fundamentally different political goals.

The reformist approach to the environment is based upon a faith in rational self-interest. Although human beings may have been blind to environmental problems for too long, once they become aware of the seriousness of the issue action will be taken. However, environmental reformism is essentially anthropocentric, it argues that environmental policies are necessary in order to satisfy the long-term needs and interests of human beings. It is therefore, typically concerned with issues that affect humans most directly, notably pollution, which damages the quality of the air we breathe, the water we drink and the food we eat, and the depletion of energy sources like coal and oil, upon which human prosperity depends. For less attention has been paid to issues like animal rights and vegetarianism. Reformist priorities are particularly apparent in relation to the question of economic growth.[25]

Rudolph Bahro for example, a leading German eco-socialist, argues that capitalism is the root cause of environmental problems. Capitalism is thus, characterised not only by class conflict but also by the progressive destruction of the natural environment. Both human labour and the natural world are exploited because they are treated simply as economic resources. Any attempt to improve the environment must therefore, involve a radical process of social change, some would say a social revolution.[26]

The essential idea of eco-socialism is that capitalism is the enemy of the environment, while socialism is its friend. Thus, the environmental problems are best tackled by abolishing capitalism or at least taming it. Bahro now argue that the ecological crisis is so pressing that it must take precedence over the class struggle.[27]

Socialists argue that socialism is naturally ecological. It's wealth is owned in common by all, it will be used in the interests of all which means in the long term interests of humanity.

Perhaps the ideology which has the best claim to being environmentally sensitive is anarchism Murray Bookchin,

American Anarchist, brought out our synthetic Environment and has rightly regarded as one of the 'founding fathers' of modern environmentalism. Bookchin has suggested that there is a clear correspondence between the ideas of anarchism and the principles of ecology. Anarchists believe in a stateless society, in which harmony develops out of mutual respect and social solidarity among human beings. The richness of such a society is founded upon its variety and diversity.[28] Anarchist communities, require no external authority or control. Bookchin has therefore likened an anarchist community to an ecosystem and suggested that both are distinguished by respect for the principles of 'diversity, balance and harmony'.

Anarchists have also advocated the construction of decentralised societies organised as a collection of communes or villages. Life in such communities is lived 'close to nature' each community attempting to achieve a high measure of self-sufficiency. Such communities would be economically diverse, they would produce food and a wide range of goods and services, and therefore contain agriculture, craftwork and small-scale industry. Self-sufficiency will make each community visibly dependent upon its natural environment, spontaneously generating an understanding of organic relationships and ecology. In Bookchin's view, decentralisation will lead to 'a more intelligent and more loving use of the environment'. A society regulated by spontaneous sympathy amongst human beings is therefore, likely to encourage an ecological balance between human beings and the natural world.[29]

4. Green Politics

The emergence of Green politics in the 1960's was part of a broader movement of ideas, commonly referred to as the New Left. The environmental movement born in the late 1960s and early 1970s was composed of radical and activist groups which sought to educate public opinion by highly-publicised campaigns of non-violent direct action.[30]

The Green movement acquired greater coherence in 1980s with the formation of Green Political parties. The environment parties of Greens was founded in Germany in 1979. Green parties have gained representation in parliaments of 10 countries, from Iceland to Portugal. In 1989 European parliament elections, Green parties won 39 seats. Green parties or environmental pressure groups are coalitions of 'light Greens' and 'dark greens' reformists and revolutionaries, conservatives and progressive. Green's parties produced not only a distinctive environmental philosophy, but also a new style of politics. 'Green politics' presents the electorate with a set of policies and priorities which clearly distinguish it from the so-called 'Grey politics' practised by other parties.[31]

Green politics is not only about warnings and threats, but it is about solutions. Policies and actions must be judged by the principle of sustainability, the capacity of a system. Sustainability sets clear limits upon human ambitions and material dreams because it requires that production does as little damage as possible to the fragile global ecosystem. Thus, the idea of 'sustainable growth' has created a radically new approach to economic policy.[32]

Ecology as Ideology

An environmental or "Green" ideology fulfills the four functions of an ideology as outlined in Chapter I. It is first of all, explanatory : it offers an explanation of how the environmental crisis came about. That crisis grew out of the human pride. The mistaken belief that human beings are self-sufficient and sovereign masters of nature. Second, the emerging "Green" ideology supplies a standard for assessing and evaluating actions, practices and policies. It applauds actions that tend to preserve and protect the natural environment—rain forests, wildlife habitats, wetlands and other ecosystems—and condemns those that damage and destroy the natural environment. Third, this ideology orients its adherents, giving them a sense of identity. Greens think of themselves as members of a species whose health and very existence is deeply dependent upon other species and upon the conditions that nourish and nurture them all. Fourth their ideology gives Greens a programme of political and social action. They assume a responsibility for among other things, promoting practices or policies that protect the natural environment.[33]

Ecology, Freedom and the Democratic Ideal

As we noted in Chapter I, every ideology subscribes to its own particular conception of freedom. The "Green" ideology is no exception. Greens believe that human beings and other species can be truly free to flourish and survive only if they overcome, both in theory and practice, the "arrogance of humanism"[34] the humanist outlook that ignores the worth of other species and their environment. Finally, as we noted in Chapter I, every modern ideology has its own characteristic interpretation of the democratic ideal. Once again, the Greens are no exception. As we saw earlier the Greens believe that each of us bears a responsibility for protecting and preserving the environment. This includes

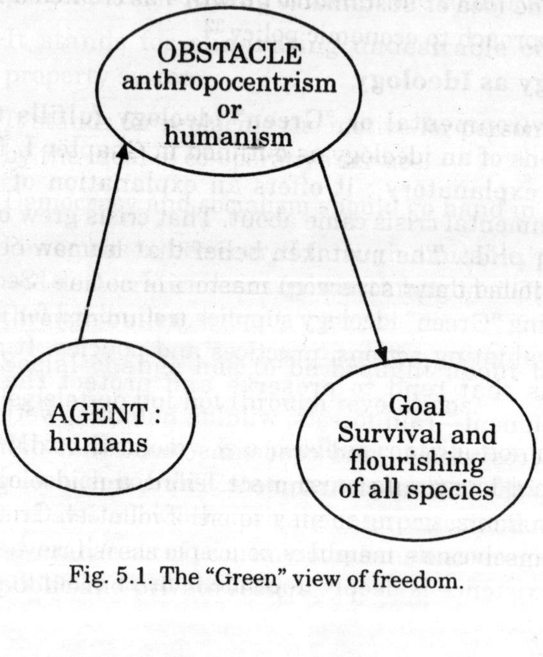

Fig. 5.1. The "Green" view of freedom.

not only the natural environment that sustain all creatures, but the social, economic, and political environment in which human beings live and work. People can flourish only within a political system that gives everyone a voice and a vote, thereby maximizing individual participation and personal responsibility.[35] That system say the Greens, is necessarily democratic. And the best kind of democracy, they add, is a decentralised "grassroots" system that encourages and permits the widest possible participation. Only in such a setting can each of us take his or her full, flair, and equal share of responsibility for preserving our planet and all its species.[36]

REFERENCES

1. All ideologies are born of crisis. The crisis out of which a broadly based Green movement has emerged is the environmental crisis. Actually, this is not a single crisis, but a series of crisis. And these crisis are interconnected.
2. Robert E. Goodin, Green Political Theory (Cambridge : Polity Press, 1992).
3. Quoted in William Leiss, The Domination of Nature (New York : George Braziller, 1972), pp. 58-59.
4. John Locke, Second Treatise of Government, para 42.
5. Marx and Engels : Basic Writings of Politics and Philosophy.
6. David Ehrenfeld, The Arrogance of Humanism (New York : Oxford University Press, 1978).
7. See in Terence Ball and Richard Dagger, eds., Ideals and Ideologies, Selection 58.
8. See, *e.g.*, Christopher Stone, Earth and other Ethics (New York : Harper and Row, 1987).
9. Hans Jonas, The Imperative Responsibility (Chicago : University of Chicago Press, 1984).
10. See Andrew Dobson, Green Political Thought (London : Unwin Hyman, 1990), pp. 206-213.

11. David Rothenberg (Cambridge : Cambridge University Press, 1989).
12. See Roderick Nash, Wilderness and the American Mind, 3rd ed. (New Haven, CT : Yale University Press, 1982), pp. 379-388.
13. Rene Dubos, The Wooing of Earth (San Francisco : North Point Press, 1981).
14. Dave Foreman, Confessions of an Eco-Warrior (New York : Harmony Books, 1991), p. 92.
15. Dave Foreman, *op. cit.*, pp. 95-100.
16. Dave Foreman, *op. cit.*, pp. 102-105.
17. Leopold, A Sand County Almanac, p. 240, also in Ideals and Ideologies, Selection 58.
18. *Ibid.*, p. 261.
19. See John Seed : Thinking like a Mountain (Philadelphia : New Society Publishers, 1988).
20. See Judith plant, ed. Healing the Wounds : The Promise of Ecofeminism (Philadelphia : New Society Publishers, 1989).
21. See Murray Bookchin, The modern Crisis (Montreal : Black Rose Books, 1986).
22. See, *e.g.*, Rudolph Bahro, Building the Green Movement (London : GRP, 1978).

23. Berry, Wendell : The Gift of Good Land, San Francisco North Point Press, 1981.
24. Bramwell, Anna, Ecology in the Twentieth Century : A History, New Haven, CT : Yale University Press, 1989.
25. Carson, Rachel, Silent Spring, Boston : Houghton Mifflin Co., 1962.
26. Catton, William R. Overshoot : The Ecological Basis of Revolutionary Change University of Illinois Press, 1980.
27. Devall, Bill and George Sessions. Deep Ecology : Living as if Nature Mattered, Layton, UT : Gibbs M. Smith, 1985.
28. Goodin, Robert E., Green Political Theory : Cambridge : Polity Press, 1992.

29. Hardin, Garrett, Filters against Folly, New York : Viking Penguin, 1985.
30. Kelly, Petra, Thinking Green, Essays on Environmentalism, Feminism, and Non-violence. Berkeley, CA : Parallax Press, 1994, p. 35-40.
31. Kelly, Petra, *op. cit.*, pp. 45-50.
32. Regan, Tom, ed., Earthbound : New Introductory Essays in Environmental Ethics. New York : Random House, 1984.
33. Sagoff, Marx, The Economy of the Earth : Philosophy, Law and the Environment, Cambridge : Cambridge University, 1988.
34. Seed John, Thinking Like a Mountain, Philadelphia, New Society Publishers, 1988.
35. Schumacher, E.F., Small Is Beautiful : Economics as if people Mattered. Garden City, NY : Doubleday Anchor, 1973.
36. Worster, Donald, Nature's Economy : A History of Ecological Ideas, 2nd ed., Cambridge : Cambridge University Press, 1994.

6

FEMINISM

1. Introduction

Until the 1960's, sexual divisions were rarely considered to be politically interesting or important.[1] If the very different social, economic and political roles of men and women were considered at all, they were usually regarded as 'natural' and therefore, as inevitable. For example, men and probably most women, accepted that some kind of sexual division of labour in society was dictated by the simple facts of biology, women were suited to a domestic and household existence by the fact that they could bear and suckle children, while the greater physical strength of men suited them to the outdoor and public world of work.[2] Conventional political theory has played its role in upholding such beliefs, usually by ignoring sexual divisions altogether. The growth of the women's movement and feminist thought. Since the 1960s has, however, severely tested such complacency. Feminists have drawn attention to sexual divisions which run through all societies, contemporary and historical, and highlighted the political significance of such divisions. In so doing, feminism has developed into a distinctive ideology, embracing concepts and theories which do not merely complement but challenge the assumptions of conventional political thought.[3]

Feminists have highlighted that they see as a political relationship between the sexes, the supremacy of men and the subjection of women in most, perhaps all, societies.[4] However, male chauvinists may also accept the fact of sexual inequality, but believe it to be an unchangeable, even desirable, feature of life. Feminism is therefore, defined by the belief that sexual inequality or oppression can and should be abolished. As such, feminism has always been linked to the women's movement, a movement which seeks to enhance the social role of women. At different times and in different places, this movement has assumed a variety of forms and pursued a diverse range of goals. It has sought to end barbaric practices like female circumcision and to abolish restrictive dress codes, struggled to achieve equal rights and wider access to education or career opportunities, it has tried to increase the number of women in elite positions in public life, and so forth. Some feminists argue that only women can genuinely sympathies with such goals because men have traditionally benefited from sexual inequality and are unlikely to act against their own interests. If this is true, men cannot be 'feminists', at best they can be 'pro-feminist' or 'anti-sexist'.[5]

Although feminism has always been associated with the women's movement, it is clearly not narrowly a 'women's issue,' rather it addresses matters of concern and significance to both sexes.[6] In particular, feminist thought seeks to broaden political understanding by exploring the cultural, social, economic and biological factors which underlie gender divisions and which therefore, condition each and every one of us, male and female. Nevertheless, it was not until the nineteenth century that an organised women's movement developed. By the mid-nineteenth century the women's movement had acquired a central focus, the campaign for female suffrage, the right to vote, which drew inspiration from the progressive extension of the franchise to men.[7] This period is usually referred to as the 'first wave' of feminism and was characterised by the demand that women should enjoy the same legal and political rights as men. Female suffrage was its principal goal because it was believed that if women could vote all other forms of sexual discrimination or prejudice would quickly disappear.[8]

The women's movement was strongest in those countries where political democracy was most advanced.[9] Women demanded the lights which in many cases their husbands and sons already enjoyed. In the United States, a women's movement emerged during the 1840s, inspired in part by the campaign to abolish slavery. The famous seneca falls convention, held in 1848, marked the birth of the American Women's Rights movement. Similar movements developed in other western countries.

'First-wave' feminism ended with the achievement of female suffrage, introduced first in New Zealand in 1893.[10] The Nineteenth Amendment of the constitution granted the vote to women in the United States in 1920. The franchise was extended to women in Britain in 1918. It was not until the 1960s that the women's movement was regenerated with the emergence of feminism's 'second wave'. The goal of 'second-wave' feminism was not merely political emancipation but 'women's liberation', reflected in the ideas of the growing Women's Liberation Movement.[11] Such a goal could not be achieved by political reforms or legal changes alone, but demanded, modern feminists argued, a radical and perhaps revolutionary process of social change.

The 1980s have sometimes been describes as a period of 'post-feminism' suggesting either that feminist goals had been achieved or that feminist political thought had lost its radical or critical edge. In the 1990's feminist organisations exist in all Western countries and women's groups have developed in the Third World, gained International Women's year in 1975 and designated the subsequent ten yeas the UN Decade for women. After the first flowering of radical feminist thought in late 1960s and early 1970s feminism has developed into a distinctive and established ideology, whose deals and values challenge the most basic assumptions of conventional political thought. However, like all other ideologies, feminism embraces a broad range of traditions and even conflicting tendencies. This does not make feminism incoherent or contradictory, but merely reflects the breadth and diversity of the modern women's movement.[12]

2. Politics of the Personal

(*a*) *Public Man, Private Woman* : Although feminist thought cuts across traditional ideologies, notably liberalism and socialism, it is based upon a distinctive set of theories and categories. The characteristic feature of feminism is that it highlights and examines gender divisions within society, and regards such divisions as political rather than natural.[13] Gender divisions are therefore, seen to reflect a 'power relationship' between men and women. Feminists question how such divisions originate and have been sustained as well as how they can be challenged and overthrown. In doing so, they have not only developed a novel account of political life and relationships, but also challenged the conventional notion of what is 'political'. In particular, feminists stress the private life, ersonal, family and sexual conduct, is highly political and is therefore, an appropriate subject for political analysis.[14]

Politics has usually been understood to be an activity which takes place within 'a public sphere' of government institutions, political parties, pressure groups and public debate. However, personal domestic and family life has normally been thought to be part of a 'private sphere' and therefore to be 'non-political'. Feminists, on the other hand, insist that politics is an activity which takes place within all social groups and not merely confines to the affairs of government or other public bodies. Politics exists wherever and whenever social conflict is found. Millett, for example, defined politics and "power structured relationships, arrangements, whereby one group of persons is controlled by another". The relationship between government and its citizens is therefore clearly political, but so is the relationship between employers and workers within a firm and also relationships in the family, between husbands and wives, and between parents and children.[15]

Traditionally, the public sphere of life, encompassing politics, work, art and literature has been the preserve of men, while women have been confined to an essentially private existence, centred upon the family and domestic responsibilities. If politics takes place only within the public sphere, the role of women and the question of sexual equality are issues of little or no political importance. Women restricted to the private roles of housewife and mother, are in effect excluded from politics.[16]

Feminists have therefore sought to breakdown the divided between 'public man' and 'private woman'.[17] But they have not always agreed about what it means to collapse the distinction between 'the public' and 'the private', or about how this can be achieved. For some feminists, emancipation consists of being able to escape from a narrowly domestic existence of home and family. Women's liberation therefore, means that women enjoy equal access with men to the public sphere, the right to an education, to pursue a career, or to enter public life. Other feminists believe that emancipation can only be achieved if some, or perhaps all, of the responsibilities of private life are transferred to the state or other public bodies—like the burden of child-rearing or the provision of nursery schools or creches at work.[18]

Female oppression is thought to operate in all walks of life and in many respects originates in the family itself. Modern feminists have therefore, been concerned to analyse what can be called 'the politics of everyday life'.

(*b*) *Patriarchy* : Feminists believe that gender, like social class, race or nation, is a significant social cleavage. Indeed, some argue that gender is the deepest and most politically important social division. Feminists have therefore, advanced a theory of 'sexual politics', in much the same way that socialist preach the ideas of 'class politics'. They also refer to 'sexism' as a form of oppression. Feminists use the concept of patriarchy to describe the power relationship between men and women. The term literally means 'rule by the father' and can refer narrowly to the supremacy of the husband father within the family, and therefore, to the subordination of both his wife and his children. In other words, some feminists preferring to use broder terms like 'male supremacy' or 'male dominance' to describe sexual relations in society at large.[19] However, feminists believe that the dominance of the father within the family symbolises male supremacy in all other institutions-in education, at work and also in politics. 'Patriarchy' therefore, commonly used in a broader sense, to mean quite simply 'rule by men' both within the family and outside. Female is controlled by men is this system. Male shall dominate female, elder male shall dominate younger. A patriarchy is therefore an hierarchic society characterised by both sexual and generational oppression.[20]

The concept of patriarchy, is nevertheless, broad.[21] Feminists may believe that men have dominated women in all societies, but accept, that the form and degree of sexual oppression has varied considerably in different cultures and at different times. At least, in western countries the social position of women has significantly improved in the twentieth century, as a result of the achievement of the vote and broader access to education, changes in marriage and divorce law, the legislation of abortion and so on. However, in parts of the third world patriarchy still assumes a cruel, even gruesome form—bride murders still occurs in India, and the persistence of the dowry system ensures that female children are often unwanted and sometimes allowed to die.[22]

Feminists disagree, however, about whether the institution of patriarchy has been universal. Some argue that ancient societies were matriarchial, system prevailed and believed in Goddess worship. Goddess worship my suggest that the female sex was respected and valued in ancient times. Traditionally, women have demanded equality with men, but equality can have very different implications. In the first place, with which men do women wish to be equal? Nineteenth century feminists were usually middle class women who wished to enjoy the privileges and rights enjoyed by their own husbands and sons, middle class men.[23] Secondly in what do women wish to be equal? Feminists are here divided. Liberal feminists argue that women should enjoy legal and political equality with men. Socialist feminists argue that equal rights may be meaningless unless women also enjoy 'social equality'— which may require the abolition of both sexual and class oppression. Thirdly, some feminists regard the very notion of equality as either misguided or simply undesirable. For many feminists 'liberation' means 'to be a women identified'.[24]

(*c*) *Sex and Gender* : 'Biology is destiny'. A women's brain may be as male chauvinists point out, smaller than a man's. Moreover, women are usually physically less powerful than men with less developed musculatures. In any case, physical hardwork, for which the male body may be better suited. Without doubt, child bearing is an attribute that is unique to the female sex, women have the capacity to suckle babies. Women may be mothers, but they need not accept the responsibilities of 'motherhood'— nurturing, educating and raising children by devoting themselves to home and family. Domestic responsibilities could be undertaken by the husband, or they could be shared equally between husbands and wives.[25]

Nevertheless, although biology may not be destiny, it cannot be denied that physical differences do exist between men and women. Sex refers to biological factors which distinguish 'men' from 'women' which are therefore, unalterable. Human nature is sexless incorporating the characteristics of both sexes. All human beings, regardless of sex, possess the genetic inheritance of a mother and a father, and therefore embody a blend of both male and female attributes or traits. Such a view accepts that sex differences are biological facts of life but insists that they have no social, political or economic significance.[26] Women and men should not be Judged by their sex, but as individuals, as 'persons'. The goal of feminism is therefore the achievement of 'personhood'. Gender differences are entirely artificial and can be obliterated.

3. Sex and Politics

Feminism is cross cutting ideology, encompassing three principle traditions, liberal, socialist, and radical. As best conservatives can argue that they support sexual equality on the ground that women's family responsibilities are every bit as important as men's public duties. Men and women are therefore 'equal but different'.

(*a*) *Liberal Feminism :* Early feminism particularly the 'first wave' of women's movement, was deeply influenced by the ideas and values of liberalism. Women's should be entitled to the same rights and privileges as men on the grounds that they were 'human beings'. She claimed that the distinction of 'sex' would become unimportant in political and social life. J.S. Mill and Harriet written in collaboration proposed that society should be organised according to the principle of 'reason' and that 'accidents of birth', such as 'sex' should be irrelevant. Liberal feminism suggests that all individuals are of equal moral worth. Individuals are entitled to equal treatment, regardless of their sex, race, colour, creed or religion. Individuals should be Judged on rational grounds on their character, on their talents or their personal worth. Any form of discrimination against women in this respect should clearly be prohibited.[27]

However, liberal feminism is essentially reformist. In reality, women are judged not only by their talents and abilities, but also by social and economic factors. Liberal feminism may therefore reflect the interests of white middle-class women in developed societies, but fail to address the problems of working class women, black women, or those in the Third World.

(*b*) *Socialist Feminism* : The central theme of socialist feminism is that patriarchy can only be understood in the light of social and economic factors. Socialist feminists have proposed that the traditional, patriarchal family should be replaced by a system of communal living and 'free love' as advocated by utopian socialists such as Fourier and Owen. In bearing and rearing children, women are producing the next generation of labour power and guaranteeing future production. Women are also responsible for socialising, conditioning and even educating children to ensure that they develop into disciplined and obedient workers.[28]

Similarly in their role as housewives, women relieve men of the burden of housework and child rearing, allowing them to concentrate their time and energy upon paid and productive employment. In that sense, the sexual division of labour between men, who undertake waged labour in factories or offices and women, who carry out unwaged domestic work, promotes economic efficiency. Furthermore, housewives are responsible for getting their husbands to work on time, properly dressed and well fed, ready for a hard day's labour or work. In the traditional family life father or husband is considered as a breadwinner and is granted leisure and relaxation at time.

Some feminists have argued that it is the unwaged nature of domestic work that accounts its low social status and leaves women financially dependent upon their husband, thereby establishing a system of social inequality women seeking liberation should recognise that the 'class war' is more important that any idea of a 'sex war'. However, modern feminists have found it increasingly difficult to accept the primacy of class politics over sexual politics. For them, sexual oppression is every bit as important as class exploitation. In Women's Estate (1971) Mitchell suggested that women fulfil four social functions : First, they are members of the workforce and are active in production, secondly, they bear children and thus reproduce the human species, thirdly, they are responsible for socialising children, and finally, they are sex objects. Liberation requires that women achieve emancipation in each of these areas, and not merely that the capitalist class system be replaced by socialism.

(*c*) *Racial Feminism :* The central feature of radical feminism is the belief thát sexual oppression is the most fundamental feature of society and that other forms of injustice—class exploitation, racial hatred and so on—are merely secondary. Gender is thought to be the deepest social cleavage and the most politically significant, more important, for example, than social class, race or nation. In 'sexual politics', Millett said, from the very early age boys and girls are encouraged to conform to very specific gender identities. This process takes place largely not only within the family, but it is also evident in literature, art, public life and the economy. Further, Millett suggests that sexual differences between meıı and women be diminished and eventually abolished.

4. Post-Feminism

Modern period has become fashionable to refer as one of 'post-feminism'. Without doubt, feminism has confronted a number of difficulties. In the first place, there are clearly splits and divisions within the women's movement, between reformist and revolutionary feminists, between radical and socialist feminists. The modern women's movement is heterogeneous and therefore, lacks a coherent or unified structure. United by a common desire to advance the role of women, feminists nevertheless disagree about how this can be achieved. Will women be liberated by the enactment of laws which guarantee equal rights or forbid sexual discrimination? Does emancipation require equal representation? Can the position of women only be advanced by a social revolution or some kind of sexual revolution?

Indeed, it merely serves to highlight the fact that feminism has developed from being a political movement into a political ideology which, like other ideologies encompasses a range of often competing traditions.[29]

The responsibility for controlling and disciplining children was placed firmly in the hands of mothers, who were 'neglecting their children'. The rise in crime and vandalism amongst young people could therefore be blamed upon working mothers, and in Britain at least, steps were taken to make parents legally and financially responsible for the actions of their children.

Finally, it has sometimes been suggested that feminist goals have largely been achieved. Just as the right to vote was won in the early years of the twentieth century, so 'second-wave' feminism has achieved the legislation of abortion in many countries, together with equal pay and anti-discrimination legislation and more easy access to political and professional life. 'New Man' who has come to terms with the 'feminine' elements in his make-up and is prepared to share domestic and family responsibilities within the 'symmetrical family'. There is undoubted evidence of the deradicalisation of the women's movement since the 1970s. The militant and revolutionary, wing of the movement has been increasingly marginalised and feminist literature reflects evidence of revisionism.

Nevertheless, the central myth of 'post-feminism', is that the most obvious forms of sexist oppression have been overcome and therefore that society is no longer patriarchal. Without doubt, for example, an increasing number of women go out to work, in many western countries a clear majority of married women. Nevertheless, they are still overwhelmingly employed in poorly paid, low status and often part-time jobs. Although legal, political and sometimes, social reforms have been introduced, a significant and substantial difference still persists between the roles of women and men in all contemporary societies. Feminism constitutes a political ideology in its own right and is unlikely to 'wither away' so long as the sexual imbalance in society persists.[30]

REFERENCES

1. De Beauvoir, S., The Second Sex, Penguin, 1972.
2. Bouchier, D., The Feminist Challenge, Macmillan, 1983.
3. Brownmiller, S., Against our Will : Men, Women and Rape, Penguin, 1976.
4. Butler, J., Gender Trouble, Chapman and Hall, 1990.
5. Charvet, J., Feminism, Dent, 1982.
6. Clarke, P. and Linzey, A., A Political Theory and Animal Rights, Pluto Press, 1990.
7. Clarke, P. and Linzey, A., *op. cit.,* pp. 45-50.
8. Coward, R., Sacred Cows : Is Feminism Relevant to the New Millennium? Harper Collins, 1999.
9. Daly, M., Ecology : The Metaethics of Radical Feminism, Beacon Press, 1978.
10. Daly, M., *op. cit.,* pp. 45-70.
11. Daly, M., *Ibid., op. cit.,* pp. 75-80.
12. Daly, M., *Ibid., op. cit.,* pp. 85-90.
13. Firestone, S., The Dialectic of Sex : The Case for Feminist Revolution, Paladin, 1970.
14. Gamble S., The Icon Critical Dictionary of Feminism and Postfeminism, Icon Books, 1999.
15. Gilman, C.P., Herald, The Women's Press, 1979.
16. Greer, G., The Female Eunuch, Paladin, 1971.
17. Greer, G., The Whole Woman, Anchor, 1999.
18. Human, M. (ed.) Feminisms : A Reader, Harvester-wheatsheaf, 1992.
19. Kemp, S.P. and Squires, J., Feminisms, Oxford University Press, 1997.
20. Millett, K., Sexual Politics, Virago, 1977.
21. Mohr, R., Justice, Columbia University Press, 1988.

22. Singer, P., Practical Ethics, 2nd eds., Cambridge University Press, 1993.
23. Spender, D., Women of Ideas (and What Men Have Done to Them) Ark, 1983.
24. Tong R., Feminist Thought : A Comprehensive Introduction, Routledge, 1992.
25. Weeks, J., Coming Out : Homosexual Politics in Britain, from the Nineteenth Century to the Present, Quarter, 1977.
26. Walter, N., The New Feminism, Little, John and Co., 1999.
27. Water, N., *Ibid., op. cit.*, pp. 40-45.
28. Walter, N., *Ibid., op. cit.*, pp. 55-60.
29. Wolf, N., Fire with Fire, Vintage, 1993.
30. Wollstonecraft, M., Vindication of the Rights of Women, Penguin, 1975.

7

ANARCHISM

1. Introduction

In every language, the word 'anarchy' often has a negative or pejorative meaning. It implies chaos and disorder, a complete breakdown of civilised and predictable behaviour. Anarchy is also linked to violence, because of a long-established public image of anarchist as a bomber or terrorist.[1] However, most anarchists would fiercely deny these associations. Anarchists do advocate the abolition of law and government. The link with violence is also misleading. At times, anarchists have openly, even proudly, supported bombings and terrorism. However, most anarchists believe violence to be mistaken and counterproductive, and many follow the ideas of Tolstoy and Gandhi and regard any form of violence as morally unacceptable.

'Anarchy' literally means "without rule". The term has been in use since the French Revolution, and was initially employed in a critical or negative sense. Proudhon proudly declared in what is property? (1940) 'I am an anarchist', that the word was clearly associated with a positive and systematic set of political ideas. However, William Godwin in his enquiring concerning political justice (1793), was produced anarchist principles.[2]

During the nineteenth century, anarchism was a significant component of a broad but growing socialist movement. Proudhon's followers joined with Marx to set up the International Workingmen's Association, or First International, in 1864. The International collapsed in 1871 because of growing antagonism between Marxists and anarchists led by Mikhail Bakunin. Syndicalism was a form of revolutionary trade unionism, popular in France, Italy and Spain. Anarcho-syndicalist movements also emerged in Latin America in the early twentieth century especially in Argentina and Uruguay and syndicalist ideas influenced. The Mexican Revolution, led by Zapata. However, the spread of authoritarianism and political repression gradually undermined anarchism in both Europe and Latin America. The Victory of General Franco in the Spanish civil war brought an end to anarchism as a mass movement. The influence of anarchism was also undermined by the success of Lenin and the Bolseviks in 1917 and the growing prestige of communism within socialist and revolutionary movements.[3]

Infact, anarchism is unusual amongst political ideologies in that it has never succeeded in winning power, at least at national level. No society or nation has therefore been modelled according to anarchist principles. It is tempting, as a result, to regard anarchism as an ideology of less significance than liberalism, socialism, conservatism or even fascism, all of which have proved themselves capable of winning power and reshaping societies.

As a political movement anarchism has suffered from three major drawbacks. First, it's goal, the overthrow of the state and all forms of political authority, is often considered to be simply unrealistic. Secondly, in opposing the state and all forms of political authority, anarchists have rejected the conventional means of exercising political influence, forming political parties, standing for elections, seeking public office, and so on. Anarchists have therefore, been forced to rely upon less orthodox methods, often based upon a faith in mass spontaneity rather than political organisation. Thirdly, anarchism does not constitute a single, coherent set of political ideas.[4]

Nevertheless, the enduring significance of anarchism is less than it has provided an ideological basis for acquiring and retaining political power, and more that it has challenged and thereby fertilised, other political creeds. Anarchists have highlighted the coercive and destructive nature of political power, and in so doing have countered statist tendencies within other ideologies, notably liberalism, socialism and also conservatism. Infact, anarchism has had growing influence upon modern political thought. Both the New Left and the New Right, for instance, exhibit libertarian tendencies, which bear the imprint of anarchist ideas. The New Left encompassed a broad range of movements, prominent in the 1960's and early 1970s, including student activism, anti-colonialism, feminism and environmentalism. The New Right also emphasises the importance of individual freedom, but believes that this can be guaranteed by market competition. Anarcho-capitalists have sought to highlight what they see as the evils of state intervention, and have been prominent in the rediscovery of free market economics.

2. Against the State

The defining feature of anarchism its opposition to the state and the accompanying institutions of government and law.[5] Anarchists have a preference for a stateless society, in which free individuals manage their affairs through voluntary agreement, without compulsion or coercion. Anarchism has a dual character, it can be thought of as both 'ultra liberalism' and 'ultra socialism'. As a result, anarchism lacks the bedrock of unifying values and principles which usually distinguish one ideology from another.

(*a*) *Political Authority :* The anarchist case against authority is that it offends against the principles of liberty and equality. Human beings are free and autonomous creatures, who should treat each other with respect and sympathy. The power of one person over another enslaves, oppresses and limits human life. It gives rise to a 'psychology of power' based upon the pattern of 'dominance and submission', a society in which, according to Paul Goodman 'many are ruthless and most live in fear'. Strictly speaking, anarchists do not object to all forms of authority; for instance, they may accept that the views of doctors or teacher is dangerous, knowledge can be abused and exploited in order to maintain the prestige of the educated over the ignorant. Anarchists are, nevertheless, firmly opposed to any form of authority which is compulsory or coercive, such as political authority, especially when it is backed up by the machinery of the modern state.[6]

All other political ideologies believe that the state fulfils some worthy or worthwhile purpose within society. Liberals think that the state is an essential guarantee of social stability and protector of individual rights. Conservatives traditionally hold that the state represents a focus for loyalty and respect within society, promoting cohesion and unity. Socialists have been seen the state as an instrument of social reform. Anarchists, however, believe that such views seriously misunderstand the nature of political authority and the state, and also fail to appreciate the negative and destructive forces which are embodied in the institutions of law and government.[7]

The state is a sovereign body, which exercises supreme authority over all individuals and associations living within a defined geographical area. As such, unlike the authority of a doctor or teacher, the authority of the state is absolute and unlimited. The authority of the state is also compulsory. Furthermore, the state is a coercive body whose laws must be obeyed because they are backed up by the threat of punishment. The state can deprive individuals of their property, their liberty and ultimately, through capital punishment, their lives. The state is also exploitative in that it robs individuals of their property through a system of taxation, once again backed up by the force of law and the possibility of punishment. Anarchists have often argued that the state acts in alliance with the wealthy and privileged and therefore serves to oppress the poor and weak. Finally, the state is destructive. 'War' as Randolph Bourne suggested, is the health of the state. Individuals are required to fight, kill and die in wars that are invariably precipitated by a quest for territorial expansion, plunder or national glory by one state at the expense of others.

Anarchists not only regard the state as evil but also believe it to be unnecessary. Hobbes said that human nature was essentially selfish, greedy and potentially aggressive. Only a sovereign state can restrain such impulses and guarantee social order. In short, order was impossible without law. Godwin, in contrast, suggested that human beings were rational and reasonable creatures. He believed that they had a natural capacity to organise their own lives in a harmonious and peaceful fashion. Indeed, he argued that it was the corrupting influence of government and unnatural laws, rather than any 'original sin' in human beings, which created injustice, greed and aggression.[8]

Anarchists have often sympathised with the famous words from Rousseau's Social Contract (1762), 'Man was born free, yet everywhere he is in chains'. Social order arises naturally and spontaneously, it does not require the machinery of law and order. Thus, anarchists who possess an essentially optimistic view of human nature.

(*b*) *The Church* : In the nineteenth century, anarchists expressed as much bitterness towards the church as they did in relation to the state. For anarchists like Proudhon or Bakunin, an anarchist political philosophy had to be based upon the rejection of Christianity. Anarchists suspected that religious and political authority usually work hand in hand. Bakunin proclaimed that, 'The abolition of the church and the state must be the first and indispensable condition of the true liberation of society. Religion is seen by anarchists as one of the pillars of the state, it propagates an ideology of obedience and submission to both spiritual leaders and earthly rulers.

Finally, religion seeks to impose a set of moral principles upon the individual and to establish a code of acceptable behaviour. Religious belief requires conformity to standards of Good and Evil, which are defined and policed by figures of religious authority, such as priests, bishops or popes. The individual is thus robbed of autonomy and the capacity to make his or her own moral judgements. Nevertheless, anarchists do not reject the religious impulse altogether. There is a clear mystical strain within anarchism. Earthly anarchists were sometimes influenced by millenarianism, a belief in the return of Christ and the establishment of the kingdom of God after 'a thousand years'.[9]

(*c*) *The Economy* : Bakunin argued that 'political power and wealth are inseparable. In the nineteenth century, anarchists usually worked with the working class movement and subscribed to a broadly socialist social philosophy. Capitalism was understood in class terms—a ruling class exploited and oppressed the masses. However, this 'ruling class' was not understood in narrow economic terms, but encompassed all those who commanded wealth, power or privilege in society. It therefore, included kings, and princes, politicians and state officials, judges and police officers, bishops and priests, as well as industrialists and bankers. Bakunin, for example, argued that in every developed society the social groups could be identified a vast majority who were exploited, a minority who were exploited but also exploited others in equal measure, and the 'supreme governing estate', a small minority of 'exploiters and oppressors pure and simple'. Anarchists identified themselves with the poor and oppressed and sought to carry out a social revolution in the name of the 'exploited masses', in which both capitalism and the state would be swept away.

3. Individuals Anarchism

The individualist tradition of anarchism has been particularly influential in the United States, where it has been supported by a political culture which emphasises rugged and self-sufficient individualism and also a deep distrust of government. The philosophical basis of individualist anarchism lies in the liberal idea of the sovereign individual. The heart of liberalism is a belief in the primacy of the individual and the central importance of individual freedom. Classical liberals understand freedom in a negative sense. It is the absence of constraints upon the individual. However, the state, by definition a sovereign, compulsory and coercive body, necessarily restricts that freedom. The individual and the state are therefore always in conflict. Quite simply, the individual cannot be sovereign in a society ruled by law and government.[10]

Although these arguments are liberal in inspiration, significant differences exist between liberalism and individualist anarchism. First, while liberals accept the importance of individual liberty, they do not believe this can be guaranteed in a stateless society. Liberal thinkers like John Locke argued that law exists to protect and enlarge liberty, rather than constrain it. Such a belief is based upon the assumption that, if not restrained by government, self-seeking individuals will abuse one another by theft, intimidation, violence and even murder. Anarchists, in contrast, believe that individuals can conduct themselves peacefully and harmoniously without the need for government to 'police' society and protect them from their fellow human beings. Anarchists differ from liberals because they believe that free individuals can live and work together constructively because they are rational and moral creatures. Reason dictates that where conflict exists it should be resolved by arbitration or debate and not by violence.[11]

Secondly, liberals believe that political power can be tamed or controlled by the development of constitutional and representative government. Constitutions seek to protect the individual by checking the power of the various institutions of government. Regular elections are designed to force a government to be accountable to the general public or at least a majority of the electorate. Anarchists dismiss the idea of a 'minimal state' or 'a democratic state'. They regard constitutionalism and democracy as simply a facade, behind which naked political oppression operates. All laws infringe individual liberty, whether the government that enacts them is constitutional or arbitrary, democratic or dictatorial. In other words, all states are an offence against individual liberty.

(*a*) *Egoism :* The term 'egoism' can have two meanings. It can suggest that individuals are essentially concerned about their ego or 'self', that they are self-interested or self seeking, an assumption that would be accepted by thinkers like Hobbes or Locke. Self-interestedness, however, can generate conflict amongst individuals and justify the existence of a state which would be needed to restrain each from harming or abusing others. However, for strainer egoism was a philosophy which placed the individual self at the centre of the moral universe. The individual, in strainer's view, should simply act as he or she chooses, without any consideration far laws, social conventions, religious or moral principles.[12]

In his most political work, Civil Disobedience (1849), Thoreau approved of Jeffer son's, liberal motto, 'that government is best which governs least', but proposed instead his own anarchist sentiment, 'That government is best which governs not at all'. For Thoreau, individualism led in the direction of civil disobedience, the individual had to be faithful to his or her conscience and do only what each believed to be right, regardless of the demand of society or the laws made by government. Thoreau's anarchism placed individual conscience above the demands of political obligation.

Benjamin Tucker took the individualist argument further by considering how autonomous individuals could live and work with one another without the danger of conflict or disorder. Two possible solutions to this problem are available to the individualist. The first emphasises human rationality and suggests that when conflicts or disagreements develop they can be resolved by reasoned discussion. The second solution was to find some sort of mechanism through which the independent actions of free individuals could be brought into harmony with one another. Warren thought that individuals had a sovereign right to the property they themselves produced and that could be exchanged for a promise to return labour in kind.

(*b*) *Anarcho-Capitalism* : Right wing libertarians like Robert Nozick, revived the idea of 'minimal state' whose principal function was the protection of individual rights. Other thinkers, such as Murray Rothbard and David Friedman, have pushed free market ideas to their limit and developed the notion of anarcho-capitalism. They believe that government can be abolished and be replaced by unregulated market competition.[13]

Anarcho-capitalists go well beyond the ideas of free market liberalism. Liberals believe that the market is an effective and efficient mechanism for delivering most goods, but argue that it also has its limits. Anarcho-capitalists, however, believe that all human wants can be satisfied by the market. Rothbard argues that profit-making protection agencies will offer a better service than the present police force because competition will provide consumers with a choice, forcing agencies to be cheap, efficient and responsive to consumer needs. Similarly, private courts will be forced to develop a reputation for fairness in order to attract custom from individuals wishing to resolve a conflict. Most importantly, unlike the authority of public bodies, the contracts thus made with private agencies will be entirely voluntary, regulated only by impersonal market forces.

4. Collectivist Anarchism

The Philosophical roots of collectivist anarchism lie in socialism rather than liberalism. Collectivism is, in essence, the belief that human beings are social animals, better suited to working together for the common good than striving for individual self interest.[14] Collectivist anarchism stresses the human capacity for individual solidarity, that human beings are naturally sociable, gregarious and co-operative. The natural and proper relationship amongst people is therefore, one of sympathy, affection and harmony. When people are linked together by a common humanity, they have no need to be regulated or controlled by government. As Bakunin proclaimed, 'Social Solidarity is the first human law, freedom is the second law'.

Anarchists are sometimes criticised for holding a naive and hopelessly optimistic view of human nature. In reality, anarchists have seldom asserted that people are 'naturally good' but rather than they have the capacity for solidarity and co-operation. If human beings are social creatures, their characters and qualities are formed by a process of social interaction and experience. Human nature is 'plastic' it is fashioned by environmental factors rather than any innate 'goodness' or 'badness'. Human beings will be greedy and aggressive if brought up in an unjust and oppressive society, but, on the other hand, they will be caring and co-operative if brought up in a society where justice and equality reign.

Peter Kropotkin, the Russian anarchist, attempted to provide a biological foundation for social solidarity in Mutual Aid (1897). Kropotkin set out to re-examine Darwin's theory of evolution, which had been used by social thinkers, such as Herbert spencer to support the idea that humankind was naturally competitive and aggressive.[15] Kropotkin did not accept that biology favoured competition and struggle, but argued instead that successful species were ones which had harnessed collective energies and possessed the capacity for 'mutual aid' or co-operation. The process of evolution had therefore, strengthened human sociability, favouring co-operation rather than competition. Kropotkin suggested that mutual aid was best reflected in the structure of city life in Ancient Greece and Medieval Europe.

(*a*) *Mutualism :* The more modest ideas of mutualism, associated with Pierre-Joseph Proudhon. In a sense, Proudhon's libertarian socialism stands between the individuals and collectivity traditions of anarchism. Proudhon came up with the famous statement that 'property is theft', and condemned a system of economic exploitation based upon the accumulation of capital. Nevertheless, unlike Marx, Proudhon was not opposed to all forms of private property. He admired the independence and initiative of small holding peasants, craftsmen and artisans. He therefore, sought a system of property ownership which would avoid exploitation and promote social harmony.[16]

Mutualism was a system of fair and equitable exchange, in which individuals or groups could bargain with one another, trading goods and services without profiteering or exploitation. Social interaction would therefore be voluntary, mutually beneficial and harmonious, requiring no regulation or interference by government. Proudhon's followed tried to put these ideas into practice by setting up mutual credit banks in France, Switzerland.

(*b*) *Anarcho-Communism :* More radically, a belief in social solidarity can lead in the direction of collectivism and communism sociable and communal existence. For example, labour is a social experience, people work in common with fellow human beings and the wealth they produce should therefore be owned in common by the community, rather than by any single individual. In this sense, property is theft, it represents the exploitation of workers who create wealth, by employers who own it. Furthermore, private property encourages selfishness and, particularly offensive to the anarchist, promotes conflict and social disharmony. Inequality in the ownership of wealth encourages greed, envy and resentment, and therefore breeds crime and disorder.

Proudhon believed that communism could only be brought about by an authoritarian state, but anarcho-communists like Kropotkin argued that true communism required the abolition of the state. Malatesta committed much of his life to anarchist agitation and the attempt to promote a peasant insurrection in his native Italy.[17] In contrast, Kropotkin spent most of his life as a writer and propagandist and tried to outline how an anarchic society ought operate. Anarcho-communists admire small self-managing communities, like the medieval city or the peasant commune. Kropotkin envisaged that an anarchic society wouid consist of a collection of largely self-sufficient—communes each owing its wealth in common. Such communes wouid be held together by the natural bonds of compassion and solidarity, rather than by regulations or laws. Kropotkin suggested that law did not prevent crime, but positively promoted it. Laws that protect private property and the government are both useless and harmful, and once political oppression and economic injustice are abolished, laws to protect the person will simply become unnecessary. Kropotkin proposed that the anti-social instincts which may live on in some individuals would be most effectively restrained by 'liberty and fraternal care'. In his view, prisons and punishment merely served to corrupt and deprave human beings, thereby promoting further crime.[18]

(*c*) *Anarchism and Marxism* : A number of obvious paralles exist between collectivity anarchism and Marxism. Both regard capitalism as a system of class exploitation and injustice. Both exhibit a preference for the collective ownership of wealth and the communal organisation of social life. Finally, both believe that a fully communist society would be anarchic. Marx expressed his this belief in the famous prediction that the state would 'wither away' once the class system was abolished. Anarchists and Marxists both stress the capacity of human-beings to order their affairs without the need for political authority.

On the other hand, there are also major differences between these two philosophies reflected in the antagonism which led to the break up of the First International in 1872. Anarchists have been critical of Marxism for a number of reasons. In the first place, anarchists have recoiled from the scientific pretensions of Marxism, in particular the idea of 'historical materialism'. Anarchists reject the central role which Marxists accord to economic life, and prefer to appeal to the utopian hopes and ideals of the masses, rather than their material or class interests. Many anarchists fear that Marxism is a form of 'economic determinism' which portrays human beings as puppets controlled by impersonal historical forces, rather than as masters of their own destiny. Secondly, anarchists have been critical of the Marxist, belief that the proletariat is the 'revolutionary class'. Anarchists believe class exploitation to be merely one form of oppression and have seen revolutionary potential in a wide variety of other social groups, including the rural peasantry, ethnic minorities, and the urban class, students and so forth. Marxists have been committed to the idea of a 'vanguard party', capable of leading the working class towards class consciousness and revolution. Anarchists, in contrast, place their face in the spontaneous instincts of masses.[19]

However, the most bitter disagreement between Marxists and anarchists centres upon their rival conceptions of their transition from capitalism to communism. In Marxist theory, the state reflects the interests of the ruling or dominant class in society. Anarchists, however, do not see the state simply as an instrument of class war they regard it as an independent and oppressive body in itself and draw no distinction between a bourgeois and proletarian state. Genuine revolution for an archist, requires not only the overthrow of capitalism, but also the immediate overthrow of all forms of state power. The state cannot be allowed to 'wither away' it must be abolished.[20]

(*d*) *Decentralisation* : It is not surprising that anarchists have little sympathy for a world divided into large nation-states. They object to all states and regard the nation as an artificial construct, far too large to be genuinely self-managing or permit each individual a direct voice in the affairs of the community. In place of political nationalism, anarchists have often been attracted to Proudhon's idea of federalism Proudhon believed that nations would break up into a confederation of self-managing regions or provinces which would co-operate with one another on the basis of voluntary and mutual agreements. Such federations would be 'topless' lacking a central authority capable of imposing its will upon the various provinces or regions. Bookchin is one of the fathers of modern environmentalism and has emphasised the need not only for human beings to live in harmony with one another, but also to live in harmony with nature.

5. Roads to Anarchy

Anarchists have been more successful in describing their ideals in books and pamphlets than they have been in putting them into practice. Quite commonly anarchists have turned away from active politics, concentrating instead upon writing or on experiments in communal or co-operative living. Anarchists have not only been a political, turning away from political life, but also positively anti-political, repelled by the conventional processes and machinery of politics. The problem confronting anarchism is that if the state is regarded as evil and oppressive any attempt to win government power or even influence government must be corrupting and unhealthy. For example, electoral politics is based upon an idea of representative democracy which anarchists firmly reject. Political power is always oppressive, regardless of whether it was acquired through the ballot box or at the point of gun. As there is no conventional 'road to anarchy' anarchists have been forced to explore less orthodox means of political activism.[21]

(*a*) *Anarcho-Syndicalism :* Syndicalism is a form of revolutionary trade unionism, drawing its name from the French word 'syndicat' meaning union or group. Syndicalism emerged first in France and was expressed by the powerful CGT union in the period before 1914. Syndicalist ideas spread to Italy, Latin America, the United States and most significantly, Spain, where they were supported by the country's largest union the CNT. Syndicalist theory drew upon socialist ideas and advanced a crude notion of class war. Workers and peasants constituted an oppressed class, and businessmen, landlords, politicians, judges and the police were their exploiters. Workers could defend themselves by organising syndicates or unions, based upon particular crafts industries or professions. In the short-term, these syndicates could act as conventional trade unions, raising wages, shortening hours and improving working conditions. However, syndicalists were also revolutionaries, who looked forward to the overthrow of capitalism and the seizure of power by the workers.

Although syndicalist theory was at times unsystematic and confused, it nevertheless exerted a strong attraction for anarchists who wished to spread their ideas among the masses. Two features of syndicalism inspired particular anarchist enthusiasm. First, syndicalists reflected conventional politics as corrupting and pointless working class power, they believed, should be exerted through direct action, boycotts, sabotage and strikes, ultimately a general strike. Secondly, anarchists saw the syndicates as a model for a decentralised, non-hierarchic society of the future.[22]

(*b*) *Violence :* The attempt to raise the masses to revolution has led some anarchists to support the use of terrorism and violence. Anarchist violence has been prominent in two periods, the late nineteenth century, reaching its peak in the 1890s and again in the 1970s. Anarchists have employed 'clandestine violence' often involving bombings or assassination, designed to create an atmosphere of terror or apprehension. The use of violence to achieve political ends has been endorsed or accepted by a variety of political groups. However, violence is usually regarded as a tactical consideration rather than an act of principle. It is a means to an end, not an end in itself. Revolutionary socialists, for example, often accept that bloodshed is regrettable but necessary feature of any successful revolution. Conservatives are prepared to allow the state to use force, especially when national security or public order is under threat. Anarchist violence, however, is different. Bombings and assassinations have been thought to be just and fair in themselves and not merely a way of exerting political influence.

Anarchists have seen violence as a form of revenge or retribution. Violence originates in oppression and exploitation, perpetrated by politicians, industrialists, judges and the police against the working masses. Anarchist violence merely mirrors the everyday violence of society and directs it towards those who are really guilty. It is a form of 'revolutionary justice'. Violence is also seen as a way of demoralizing the ruling classes, encouraging them to loosen their grip upon power and privilege. Finally, violence is a way of raising political consciousness and stimulating the masses to revolt.

In practice, anarchist violence has been at best, counter productive. Far from awakening the masses to the reality of their oppression, political violence has normally provoked public horror and outrage. There is little doubt that the association between anarchism and violence has damaged the popular appeal of the ideology. Furthermore, violence seems an uncompromising way of persuading the ruling class to relinquish power.

(c) *Pacifism :* In practice, most anarchists see violence as tactically misguided, others regard it as abhorrent in principle. These latter anarchists have often been attracted to the principles of non-violence and pacifism developed by Leo Tolstoy and Mahatma Gandhi, both of whom expressed ideas sympathetic to anarchism. In his novels and political writings, Tolstoy developed the image of a corrupt and false modern civilisation. Communes were founded to spread Tolstoy's teachings, central to which was the principle of non-violence.[23]

Gandhi campaigned against racial discrimination and led the movement for Indian independence from Britain eventually granted in 1947. His political method was based upon the idea of 'satyagraha' or nonviolent resistance, influenced both by the teachings of Tolstoy and Hindu religious principles. His ideal community was the traditional Indian village, a society both self governing and largely self-sufficient. Its symbol, the spinning wheel, which was both the source of its livelihood and a mark of its independence, has been incorporated into the Indian flag.

The principle of non-violence was crucial to Gandhi's philosophy for two reasons. First, it reflected the sanctity of all human life, indeed of all living beings. A society regulated by love must for Gandhi, be based upon compassion and respect. Secondly, non-violence was a political strategy. In the campaign against British rule, non-violent resistance was a powerful weapon, mobilising popular support for independence within India itself and around the world. Anarchists who have been attracted to the principles of pacifism.[24]

REFERENCES

1. Apter, D. and Joll, J. (eds.), Anarchism Today, Macmillan, 1971.
2. Bakunin, M., Bakunin on Anarchism, ed., S. Dolgoff, Black Rose Books, 1980.
3. Bakunin, M., Statism and Anarchy, Cambridge University Press, 1990.
4. Bookchin, M., Post-Scarcity Anarchism, Wildwood House, 1974.
5. Bowen J. and Purkis, J., Twenty-first Century Anarchism, Cassell, 1997.
6. Carter, A., The Political Theory of Anarchism, Routledge and Kegan Paul, 1971.
7. Edwards S. (ed.,) Selected Writings of Pierre-Joseph Proudhon, Macmillan, 1969.
8. Friedman D., The Machinery of Freedom, Harper, 1973.
9. Godwin, W., An Enquiry Concering Political Justice, Penguin, 1976.
10. Hamilton, A., *et al.*, The Federalist Papers, Mentor Books, 1961 (1788).
11. Illich, I., Deschooling Society, Penguin, 1970.
12. Kropotkin P., Mutual Aid, Heinemann, 1910.
13. Marshall P., Demanding the Impossible : A history of Anarchism, Fontana, 1993.
14. Miller D., Anarchism, Dent, 1984.
15. Nozick, R., Anarchy, State and Utopia, Blackwell, 1974.
16. Porritt, J. and Winner D., The Coming of the Greens, Fontana, 1988.
17. Proudhon, P. J., General Idea of the Revolution in the Nineteenth Century, Freedom Press, 1923.
18. Rothbart, M.N., For Anew Liberty : The Libertarian Manifesto, Collier, 1978 (1973).

19. Stirner, M., The Ego and His Own, Cape, 1921 (1844).
20. Thoreau, H.D., The Duty of Civil Disobedience, Signet, 1960 (1849).
21. Ward, C., Anarchy in Action.
22. Warren J., Equitable Commerce, Fowler and Wells, 1852.
23. Woodcock, G., Anarchism, Penguin, 1963.
24. Woodcock, G., The Anarchist Reader, Fontana, 1977.

8

LIBERALISM

HISTORICAL BACKGROUND

Ancient Origins

For more than 300 years, the hallmark of liberalism has been the attempt to promote individual liberty. The word liberal and liberty both derive from the Latin liber, meaning free. "Liberal" did not enter the vocabulary of politics until early in the nineteenth century, however, long after "liberty" was widelyssed as a political term. Before the nineteenth century, "liberal" was commonly used to mean generous or tolerant—an attitude that supposedly benefit a "gentleman", just as a "Liberal education" was meant to prepare a young gentlemen for life. "Liberal" still means generous or tolerant, of course, as when someone says that a teacher follows a liberal grading policy or a child has liberal parents. But now-a-days through an extension of this common use, "liberal" more often refers to a political position or point of view.[1]

The first clear sign of this political use occurred in the early 1800s when a faction of the Spanish legislature adopted the name Liberalies. From there the term travelled to France and Great Britain, where the party known as the Whigs evolved by the 1840s into the Liberal Party. These early liberals shared a desire for a more open and tolerant society—one in which people would be free to pursue their own ideas and interests with as little interference as possible. A liberal society was to be in short, a free society.

But what makes a society free? What is freedom and how can we best promote it? These questions providing the grounds not only for the arguments among liberals, but also for disputes between liberalism and other ideologies.[2]

In the case of liberalism, the emphasis on individual liberty rests on a conception of human-beings as fundamentally rational individuals. Liberals acknowledge that people do have passions and desires, but they maintain that we also have the ability, through reason, to direct and control our desires. Most women and men, they insist, are rational beings who know what is in their own interests and given the opportunity, are capable of acting to promote them. Liberals generally agree that self-interest is primary motive for most people. Some argue that self-interest should be given free rein, while others, respond that it should be carefully directed to promote the good of all, most hold that it is wisest to think of people as beings who are more interested in their own good than the well-being of others. This implies, inturn, that all these rational, self-interested men and women will find themselves competing with one another in their attempts to promote their personal interests. This is healthy, liberals say, as long as the competition remains fair and stays within proper bounds. Exactly what is fair and where these proper bounds lie is a subject of sharp disagreement among liberals, as is the question of how best to promote competition. For the most part, though liberals are inclined to regard competition as a natural part of the human condition.[3]

On the liberal view, then human beings are typically rational self-interested and competitive. This implies that they are capable of living freely, but what does it mean to live in this vay. How, that is, do liberals conceive of freedom? To answer this, let us employ the model depicting freedom as a triadic relationship involving an agent who is free from some obstacle to pursue some goal. In the case of liberalism, the agent is the individual. Liberals want to promote the freedom of no particular group or class of people, but of each and every person as an individual. To do this, they have sought to free people from a variety of restrictions or obstacles. In the beginning, liberals were most concerned with removing social and legal barriers to individual liberty especially social customs, ties of fendal dependence and religious, conformty. Since then other liberals have claimed that poverty, racial and sexual prejudice, ignorance, and illness are also obstacles to individual liberty. But in spite of these differences, liberals agree that the individual must be free to decide for himself and more recently, herself—what goals to pursue in life. Most liberals have believed, that is, that the individual is the best judge of what is in his or her interest, so each person ought to be free to live as he or she sees fit—as long as the person does not choose to interfere with other's freedom to live as they see fit.[4]

This suggests that equality is also an important element in the liberal conception of freedom.[5] In the liberal view, each person is to have an equal opportunity to enjoy liberty. No persons liberty is more important or valuable than any others. This does not mean that everyone is to be equally successful or to have an equal share of the good things of life, whatever they may be. Liberals do not believe that everyone can or should be equally successful, but that everyone should have an equal chance to succeed. Liberalism thus stresses competition, for it wants individuals to be free to compete, on an equal footing, for what ever they count as success. Anything that prevents a person from having an equal opportunity—whether it be privileges for the aristocracy, monopolies that block economic competition, or discrimination based on race, religion, or gender—can be an obstacle to a person's freedom that ought to be removed.[6]

Liberalism, in short, promotes individual liberty by trying to guarantee equality of opportunity within a tolerant society. In the English-speaking world, these ideas are so much a part of our lives and our thinking this they seem natural. But this is because these liberal ideas are so much a part of our lives and our thinking that they seem natural. But this is because these liberal ideas are so much a part of our heritage in the English-speaking world and throughout Western civilization in general. These ideas were not always taken for granted, however, not even in England and Europe.

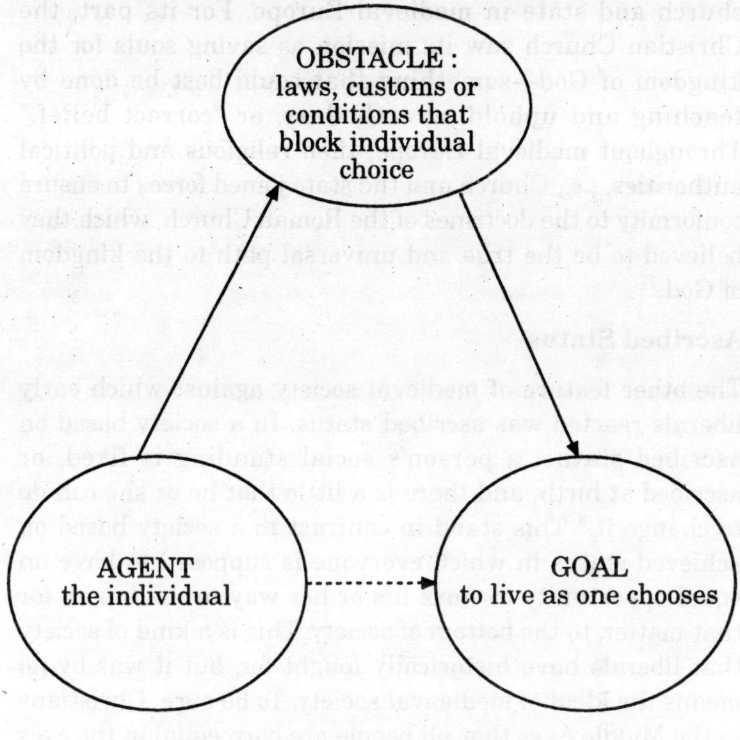

Fig. 8.1. The liberal view of freedom.

HISTORICAL BACKGROUND

Medieval Origins

The origins of liberalism can be traced to a reaction against two of the characteristic features of medieval society in Europe—religious conformity and ascribed status. This reaction, which developed over the course of centuries, took different forms in different times and places.

Religious Conformity

This view point called for freedom of religion and separation of church and state. These ideas were foreign to the dominant ways of thinking in the Middle Ages, when church and state were supposed to be partners in the defense of Christendom. Indeed, there was no clear distinction between church and state in medieval Europe. For its part, the Christian Church saw its mission as saving souls for the kingdom of God—something that could best be done by teaching and upholding orthodoxy, or "correct belief." Throughout medieval Europe, then religious and political authorities, *i.e.,* Church and the state joined forces to ensure conformity to the doctrines of the Roman Church, which they believed to be the true and universal path to the kingdom of God.[7]

Ascribed Status

The other feature of medieval society against which early liberals reacted was ascribed status. In a society based on ascribed status, a person's social standing is fixed, or ascribed at birth, and there is a little that he or she can do to change it.[8] This stand in contrast to a society based on achieved status in which everyone is supposed to have an equal opportunity to work his or her way to the top or, for that matter, to the bottom of society. This is a kind of society that liberals have historically fought for, but it was by no means the ideal of medieaval society. To be sure, Christians in the Middle Ages that all people are born equal in the eyes of God, but this was compatible in their eyes with great inequalities in life here on earth. What counted was the state of one's soul, not one's status in society.

Yet status mattered very much in earthly life, for one's position and prospects were fixed by his or her social "rank", "order" or "estate."[9] This was especially true under feudalism. Under feudalism, an intricate web of relationships developed in which one knight, the lord, would give the use of land to a lesser knight, the vassal. In the beginning the original lord retained ownership of the land, with the vassal receiving only the right to use it and enjoy its fruits. These relationships gradually became hereditary, however, leading to a complicated network of ranks, status and loyalties. In one respect, though, feudalism simplified matters by reinforcing the existing tendency to divide society into two broad classes of people down the generations, a distinct class of land-owning nobles or aristocrats took shape. These nobles thought themselves naturally superior to the commoners, who were the great majority of the people. They also believed that their noble birth entitled them to exercise authority over the commoners and to enjoy privileges and liberties unavailable to common men and women.[10]

This emphasis on social "rank", or "estate" was reflected in the parliaments or estates—general that began to appear in the late Middle Ages. Serfs (from the latin word serves, slave) were commoners, but they were not free. They were peasants, or agricultural labourers. Unlike free peasants, the serfs owned no land. Instead, they farmed plots owned by the lord of the manor, and from their plots, they had to provide for their families and pay rent to the lord, typically in the form of crops.[11]

The most distinctive feature of serfdom, however, was the serf's lack of freedom to choose where to live and what work to do. Serfs were often legally attached to the land or the person of the lord. By custom and law they were bound—hence the term, bondsman—either to remain on and work the land where they were born or, if attached to a person, to serve the lord wherever required. In exchange, serfs received protection from the lord. If they thought this is a poor bargain, there was nothing they could do as a rule, to earn release from serfdom. Some tried to win their freedom by force of arms, others ran away to the towns and cities and still others accepted their condition as part of the natural course of life; although perhaps cherishing a hope that their lord might some day free them.[12]

Whether a serf, a noble or a free commoner, then, a person was born into a certain rank or estate in medieaval Europe and could do little to change it. The Church provided an exception to this rule, for people from all ranks of society could hope to find a place among the clergy. In other respects, though medieval Society was firmly rooted in ascribed status. Nobles were those born into the nobility, while the children of free commoners and serfs were virtually locked into the social position of their parents, and no amount of effort or ability could significantly improve their stations in life. Even freedom was a matter of social position.[13]

Against this society rooted in ascribed status and religious conformity, liberalism emerged as the first distinctive political ideology. But this reaction did not take definite shape until a number of social, economic and cultural changes disturbed the medieval order. Many of these were directly related to the out burst of creativity in the fourteenth and fifteenth centuries known as the Renaissance. The expansion of trade and commerce in the late Middle Ages played a part in the breakdown of the Medieval order too. Columbus's attempt to find a new trade route to Asia is noteworthy in this regard, for he discovered what was, for Europeans, an entirely new world—a New World that became a symbols of great new possibilities. But of all the historical developments that contributed to the decline of the medieaval order and the rise of liberalism, the most important was the protestant reformation.

Quite unintentionally, the protestant reformers prepared the way for liberalism. By teaching that salvation comes through faith alone, Luther (1483–1546) was a priest and professor of theology at the University of Wittenberg, and the other reformers encouraged people to value individual conscience more than the presentation of unity and orthodoxy. From individual conscience to individual liberty was still a radical step for the time, but it was a step that the early liberals took. Thus, liberalism began as an attempt to free individuals from the constraints of religious conformity and ascribed status. It also began, as most ideologies have begun, as an attempt to bring about a fundamental transformation of society. It was, in short, revolutionary.

LIBERALISM AND REVOLUTION

England

After defeating the Spanish Armada in 1588, England entered the seventeenth century more secure and powerful than it had ever been. Queen Elizabeth I was on the throne and William Shakespeare was writing plays. Then came contributions to literature by John Donne and John Milton, to Philosophy by Thomas Hobbes and John Locke, and to science by Isaac Newton and William Harvey, the physician who discovered the circulation of blood. And commerce and exploration flourished as English colonies sprang up in North America and India.

But the seventeenth century was also a time of turmoil for England. Elizabeth was succeeded in 1603 by a distant cousin, James Stuart, king of Scotland. The new king soon found himself engaged in a power struggle with parliament. In 1642 the conflict erupted into civil war. The war between Crown and Parliament was further fueled by religious, social and economic elements. For many people the war was primarily a religious conflict. The social and economic divisions are less clear, but it seems that the land-owning aristocracy supported the king while the middle class the "gentlemen", landowners and the merchants-generally sided with parliament.

In this war, pen and ink played as great a part as bullets and swords. From every side came a vast outpouring of pamphlets, treatises, sermons, and even major works of political theory. Now we must take note of the first major work of political philosophy to bear the distinctive stamp of liberalism, Thomas Hobbes Leviathan. Hobbes (1588-1679) write Leviathan in France, where he had fled to avoid the war, and published it in 1651 two years after the beheading of Charles I brought the war to an end. There was nothing new in the conclusion he reached in Leviathan. Like St. Paul and many others, Hobbes maintained that the people of a country should obey those who have power over them. But he refused to base this conclusion on the simple claim that this was God's Will. Even though Hobbes cited scripture, his argument was fundamentally secular—and, he thought, "scientific"—as it was based on self-interest rather than divine commands.[14]

Thomas Hobbes (1588-1679)

According to Hobbes, the individual should obey whoever is in power, as long as the person or persons in power protect him or her. To provide protection or security is the only reason for government in the first place. And to prove his point Hobbes asked his readers to imagine that they were in a state of nature with no one having authority over them. In such a state, he said all individuals are equal—no one is born to hold a higher rank or status than anyone else—and have a natural right to do as they wish. The problem is human nature. There is a perpetual desire for power. The perpetual and the relentless desire for power leads individuals into conflict with one another and turns the state of nature into a "war of every man against every man" where life can be nothing but "solitary, poor, nasty, brutish and short."[15]

Nothing, in Hobbes's view, could be worse than this. So the fearful and rational individuals in the state of nature enter into a social contract to establish political authority. To provide for their security, they surrender all but one of their rights—the right to defend themselves—to those to whom they grant authority. On Hobbes's argument, then, government is founded in the consent of the people. But by their consent, the people authorize to sovereign—the person or persons in power—to do anything necessary to maintain peace and order. This includes the power to force everyone to worship as the sovereign requires, for Hobbes saw religious differences as one of the leading sources of conflict. For the sake of security, then, the people grant the sovereign absolute, unlimited power, retaining only the right of defend themselves when the sovereign directly threatens them.

Given this conclusion, the claim that Leviathan bears the distinctive stamp of liberalism may seem odd. Liberals certainly have not made a habit of supporting absolute rulers or enforcing religious conformity. What gives Hobbes's theory the stamp of liberalism is not his conclusion, however, but his premises. Individuals are equals, on Hobbes's account, and everyone has a natural right to be free. They create government through their consent in order to protect their interests. In these respects, Hobbes's position is very much that of a liberal or, as some prefer to say, a protoliberal that is, one who articulated the main premises of an emerging liberal ideology. It remained for John Locke to use these premises to reach conclusions that were definitely liberal.

Locke (1632-1704) was 16 years old when Charles I beheaded and parliament abolished the monarchy. Locke completed the Two Treatises while in exile in Holland, where he had fled for safety in 1683. In Holland, then the most tolerant country in Europe, Locke also wrote his letter concerning Toleration. Both works were published in England after the Glorious Revolution of 1688 forced James II, to flee to France. James's daughter Mary and her husband William, prince of Orange (in the Netherlands), became England's new monarchs. All these developments were much to Locke's liking. In the letter concerning Toleration, he argued that it is wrong for governments to force their subjects to conform to a particular religion. Drawing a distinction between private and public matters, Locke said that religious belief is normally a private concern and not a proper subject for government interference. Governments should tolerate diverse religious beliefs unless the practice of those beliefs directly threatens the public order. But Catholicism should not be tolerated for exactly this reason. Catholics owe their first loyalty a foreign monarch, the pope, so they cannot be trustworthy members of a commonwealth. Locke also denied toleration to atheists for a similar reason, claiming that anyone who denied the existence of God, salvation, and damnation could not be trusted at all. If, these seem severe restrictions by our standards, they were nonetheless quite liberal, even radical, by the standards of Locke's time.

John Locke (1632-1704)

Important as his argument for toleration was, Locke's theory of political authority in the second of his Two Treatises of Government marked an even more important milestone in the development of liberalism. Locke's purpose in the Second Treatise was much the same as Hobbes's in Leviathan—to establish the true basis for political authority or government and in several crucial respects his premises resemble Hobbess. He began his argument, as Hobbes did, with the state of nature, where everyone is free and equal. There is no ascribed status in this state of nature. There are natural rights—the right to life, liberty and property Locke referred.[16] The rights a person may surrender or forfeit—by attacking others, for instance, a person may, forfeit his right to life or liberty but no one can simply take them away.

Unlike Hobbes's state of nature, Locke's is not a state of war. It is "inconvenient", however, largely because so many people are unwillingly to respect the rights of others. Recognizing this difficulty, people in the state of nature enter into a social contract to establish a political society with laws and a government to make, interpret, and enforce them. But we should remember, Locke said, that people create government to do a job—to protect their natural rights. The government has authority, therefore, only in so far it does what it needs to do to preserve the lives, liberty and property of its subjects. If the government begins to violate these rights by depriving its subjects of life, liberty and property—then the people have the right to overview the government and establish a new one on its place.

Although he began with premises very similar to Hobbes's, Locke reached a very different conclusion. Both denied that social status was somehow fixed or ascribed by nature, and both believed that government is founded on the consent of the people, but Locke believed that people can consent to create and obey only a limited or constitutional government. To give anyone total and absolute power over our lives would be both irrational and contrary to the will of God. Both also believed that people have natural rights, but for Locke this included a right to worship as one chose within limits, and a right of revolution—a right that would be invoked four score and six years after the publication of the Two Treatises of Government in the American Declaration of Independence.

The most thorough and influential defense of Laissez faire was Adam Smith's Inquiry into the Nature and Causes of the Wealth of Nations (1776). Laissez faire means let it be, leave it alone. Smith (1723-1790), a Scottish philosopher, agreed with the physiocrat's attack on mercantilism and monopoly. Far from serving the public interest, Smith said, restraints on economic competition serve only the interests of those few people who are able to take advantage of them.[17] For most people, lack of competition simply means higher prices and scarcer goods.

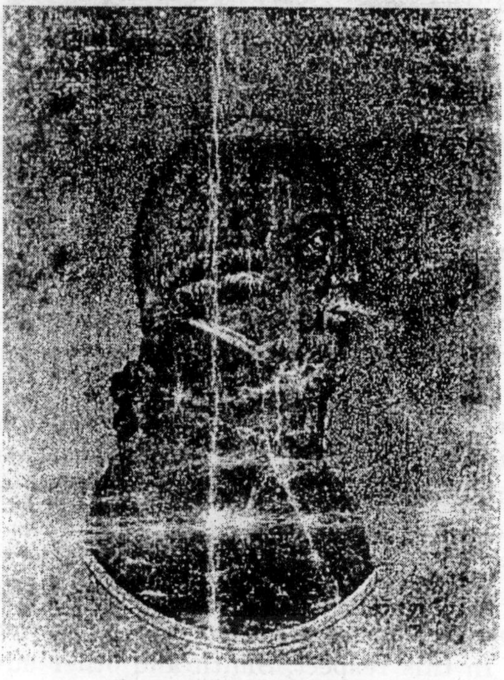

Adam Smith (1723-1790)

To remedy this, Smith recommended an economic policy that would allow individuals to compete freely in the market place. Not only will this be the fairest policy, since it gives everyone an equal opportunity, but it will also be the most efficient. For there is nothing like self-interest in this case, the desire for profits to motivate people to provide the goods and services that others want. Smith reasoned that removing economic restrictions and privileges will encourage people to produce and sell goods for a profit. In order to turn a profit, producers will have to produce either a better or a cheaper good than their competitors, otherwise, people will not buy their products. Private interest, set free, will thus indirectly promote the public good by making available more and better and cheaper goods.

Smith also argued, against the mercantilists, for free trade between countries. If people in some foreign land can sell us something we want for less than it costs to produce it ourselves then let them do it. High taxes on foreign imports may encourage industry at home, Smith said, but it does so at great cost to the consumer, who has fewer and more expensive goods available. In the long run, peaceful and unrestricted trade between countries benefits everyone.

From Smith's point of view, then government should have as little as possible to do with economic exchanges. Government has only three proper functions, he said. First, it must defend the country against invasion. Second, it must promote justice—mostly by protecting property rights—and maintain order. Finally, it must provide certain public works and institutions that private enterprise will not provide, such as roads, bridges, canals, and harbors (what economists now term the "infrastructure" necessary to the conduct of business), as well as public education. All other matters are best left to the private business of self-interested individuals, who should be free to make their way in the world as they see fit. In this respect, Smith and other advocates of capitalism have taken a liberal position.

UTILITARIANISM

Jeremy Bentham

The original leader of Utilitarians (or philosophic Radicals) was the English philosopher Jeremy Bentham (1748-1832). Society should be reformed to make it more rational, he insisted, and the first step in this direction is to recognize that people act out of self-interest. Moreover, everyone has an interest in experiencing pleasure and avoiding pain. As Bentham put it, "Nature has placed mankind under the governance of two sovereign masters, pleasure and pain. It is for them alone to point out what we ought to do, as well as to determine what we shall do." This is simply a fact of human nature, he thought and there is nothing we can do to change it. But once we understand that all people seek pleasure and avoid pain in everything they do, we can take steps to be better pleasure—seekers and pain—avoiders.[18]

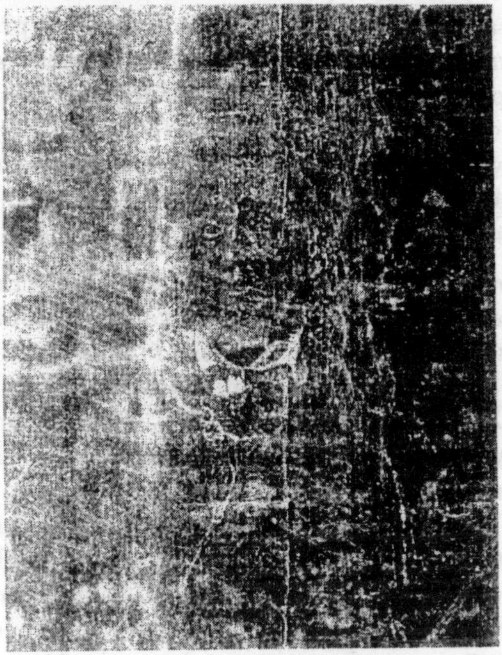

Jeremy Bentham (1748–1832)

Bentham did not mean that we should seek pleasure in immediate gratification in getting drunk, for example- because the pain we or others suffer later will probably outweigh the short-term pleasure. He meant rather, that we should seek utility. Something has utility—a hammer for a carpenter, for instance, or money for almost everyone–if it helps someone do what he or she wants. Since people want to be happy, utility promotes happiness. This led Bentham to argue that everyone should follow the principle of utility—

do whatever will produce the greatest happiness of the greatest number.

Bentham recognized that people will sometimes fail to see what does and does not have utility for them—someone who drops out of school may not appreciate the utility of education; for example. He also admitted that, in pursuing our own pleasures, we may bring pain to others. But the purpose of government is to solve these problems. In Bentham's words, "The business of government is to promote the happiness of society, by punishing and rewarding". By punishing those who cause pain to others and by rewarding those who give pleasure, in other words, government can and should act to promote the greatest happiness of the greatest number.

From this Bentham drew two general conclusions about government. The first was that government could generally promote the greatest happiness of the greatest number simply by leaving people alone. Individuals are usually the best judges of their own interests, so government should usually let people act as they see fit. For this reason, Bentham accepted the Laissez-faire arguments of Adam Smith. His second conclusion was that government is not likely to promote the greatest happiness of the greatest number of it is controlled by a small segment of society. In the pursuit of utility, Bentham declared, everyone is to count equally. Government must weigh everyone's interests and this requires that almost everyone be allowed to vote. Although Bentham's views on voting are not altogether clear, he did support universal male suffrage and, with certain reservations, the vote for women as well.[19]

John Stuart Mill

The views of John Stuart Mill (1806-1873) on this matter are not in doubt, for Mill was an ardent advocate of women's rights. An influential utilitarian, Mill was the leading liberal philosopher of the nineteenth century. Whether supporting women's rights or arguing that government should set minimum educational standards for all, Mills greatest concern was to defend and extend individual liberty. This is most evident in his essay On Liberty.[20]

When Mill published on Liberty in 1859, liberalism seemed to have triumphed, at least in England and the United States. The old enemies ascribed status, religious conformity, and absolute government—were no longer the obstacles to individual liberty they had been. Yet, Mill was alarmed by what he took to be a new threat to liberty in the growing power of public opinion. In the olden days, Mill said, the chief enemy of freedom was the government, but now that we elect representatives, the government is more responsive to the desires of the people. It is responsive however, to the majority of the people, or at least the majority of those who vote, and this allows them to use the government to restrict or take away the liberty of those who do not share the majority's views. Mill was worried about "the tyranny of the majority."

On liberty was Mill's attempt to deal with this new form of tyranny. He says, every one should be free to do whatever he or she wants so long as his or her actions do not harm or threaten to harm others. Government and society, then should not interfere with an individual's activities unless that individual is somehow harming or threatening to harm others. Government has no business prohibiting the sale of alcohol, for instance, on the grounds that drinking harms the drinker, but government should certainly prohibit drunken driving on the grounds that this poses a serious threat of harm to others.

Mill defended his principle by appealing not to natural rights as most of the early liberals had done, but to utility. Freedom is good thing, he argued, because it promotes "the permanent interests of man as progressive being". He meant by this that both individuals and society as a whole will benefit if people are encouraged to think and act freely. For

John Stuart Mill (1806-1873)

the individual, freedom is vital to personal development. Our mental and moral faculties are like muscles Mill said, Without exercise, they will weaken and shrivel. But people cannot exercise their minds and their powers of judgement when they are constantly told what they can and cannot do. To be fully human, then, individuals must be free to think and speak for themselves as long as they neither harm nor threaten harm to others.[21]

It is possible, of course, that the people who speak and act freely will make others, perhaps even the majority of society, uncomfortable and unhappy. But in the long run, Mill argued, the ideas of nonconformists such as Socrates, Jesus, and Galileo work to the benefit of society. Progress is possible only when there is open competition between different ideas opinions, and beliefs. As in economics, a free market place of ideas, yields a greater variety to choose from and allows people to distinguish good ideas from bad.

Without freedom of thought and action, society will remain stuck in the rut of conformity and never progress. [22]

Mill's desire to promote individual liberty also led him to recommend representative democracy as the best possible form of government.[23] In considerations on Representative Government (1861) he maintained that the political participation was one of the best forms of exercise for the mental and moral faculties. And only in a democracy is this kind of exercise available to all citizens. Even so, Mill's fear of "the tyranny of the majority" kept him from embracing democracy wholeheartedly. Among other things, he favoured a form of plural voting in which every man and woman will have a vote, but some those with higher levels of education, for instance—will have two, three, or more. Plural voting thus would enable everyone to enjoy the benefits of political participation, yet allow more enlightened and better informed citizens to protect individual liberty. Such a system was necessary, Mill believed, at least until the overall level of education was high enough to remove the threat of majority tyranny.[24]

As for economic matters, Mill began his career as a staunch defender of Laissez-faire capitalism. Towards the end of his life, however, he called himself a socialist. This shift in his thinking was one of the first signs of an even greater shift on the part of many liberals in the latter part of the nineteenth century—a shift that divided liberalism into rival camps.[25]

Neoclassical Liberalism

Since the second half of the nineteenth century, neoclassical liberals have consistently argued that government should be as small as possible in order to leave room for the exercise of individual freedom. The state or government should be nothing more than a "night watchman" whose only legitimate business is to protect the person and property of individuals against force and fraud.[26] Some neoclassical, liberals have based this argument on an appeal to natural rights, others on an appeal to utility. In the late 1800s, however, the most influential among them based their arguments on Darwin's theory of evolution.

In his Origin of Species (1859) Charles Darwin used the idea of "natural selection" to account for the evolution of life forms. Darwin held that individual creatures within every species experience random mutations, or accidental changes, in their biological makeup. Some mutations enhance a creature's ability to find food and survive, while others do not. Those lucky enough to have beneficial mutations are more likely to survive—and to pass these biological changes along to their offspring—than less fortune members of their species. Thus nature "selected" certain creatures with certain mutations and thereby "directed" the path of evolution. But all this was accidental and unintentional. The biological good fortune also puts the members of some species at an advantage over others in competition for food—for instance, giraffes are able to eat the leaves on the higher branches of trees, which is distinct advantage when food is scarce. Mutations thus account not only for the evolution of species, but also for their survival or extinction.[27]

Social Darwinism

Herbert Spencer (1820-1903), an English philosopher, had begun to think in evolutionary terms even before Darwin's Origin of Species appeared and he took Darwin's work to confirm the main lines of his own thought. In particular, spencer claimed that there is a natural struggle for survival within the human species. Nature means for individuals to be free to compete with one another. Those who are strongest, smartest, and most fit for this competition will succeeds and prosper, those who are unfit will fail and suffer. But this is simply nature's way, spencer said. Helping the poor and the weak impedes individual freedom and retards social progress by holding the strong back. Indeed, it was spencer who coined the phrase, "survival of the fittest".[28] Such views made spencer a leading advocate of the "night watchman state".

William Graham Summer (1840-1910) was the leading American advocate of Social Darwinism. A professor at Yale University, Sumner proclaimed that "there are two chief things with which government has to deal. They are, the property of men and the honour of women". These are the only matters with which government should concern itself. In the competition of survival, government should simply see to it that everyone competes fairly and freely. As summer put it, "A drunkard in the gutter is just where he ought to be, according to the fitness and tendency of things. Nature has set up on him the process of decline and dissolution by which she removes things which have (outlived) their usefulness".[29]

Welfare Liberalism

Like classical and neoclassical liberals, welfare liberals believe in the value of individual liberty. But welfare liberals maintain that government is not just a necessary evil.[30] On the contrary, properly directed, government can be a positive force for promoting individual liberty by ensuring that everyone enjoys and equal opportunity in life.

T.H. Green

One of the first to make the case for welfare liberalism was T.H. Green (1836-1882), a professor of philosophy of Oxford University. The heart of liberalism, Green said, has always been the desire to remove obstacles that block the free growth and development of individuals. In the past that meant limiting the powers of government so that people can be free to live, worship, and compete in the market place as they see fit.[31] By the mid, 1800s these aims had largely been accomplished in countries like England, and it was time to recognize and overcome still other obstacles to freedom and opportunity—obstacles like poverty and illness, prejudice and ignorance. To overcome these obstacles, green argued, it was necessary to enlist the power of the state.[32]

Green based his argument on a distinction between two different ways of thinking about freedom, ways that he called negative and positive freedom. The early liberals, regarded freedom as a negative thing, he said, for they thought of freedom as the absence of restraint. Someone who was restrained—tied up and locked in Jail, for instance—was not free, while someone who was unrestrained was.[33] But Green believed that there is more to freedom than this. Freedom is not merely a matter of being left alone, it is the positive power or ability to do something. Thus, we may say that a child born into poverty, with no real opportunity to escape, is not truly free to grow and develop to the full extent of his or her abilities. Even if no one is intentionally restraining that child by keeping him or her in poverty, the child is still not free. Green argued, any one who values individual liberty will want to take steps to overcome those circumstances that are such formidable obstacles to freedom.[34]

Green and other welfare liberals believed that society, acting through government, should establish public schools and hospitals, aid the needy, and regulate working conditions to promote worker's health and well-being. Only through such public support would the poor and powerless members of society become truly free. Green responded that everyone gained freedom when he or she served the common good. For positive freedom is the ability to realize or achieve our ideal or "higher" selves in co-operation with others.[35] Human beings are not merely pleasure—seekers and pain avoiders. We have higher ideals, including ideals of what we can and ought to be as persons. The laws and programmes that help the unfortunate, smooth social relations, and restrict all-out competition are positive aids to liberty, not restraints that limit our freedom. They may restrict over selfish or "lower" selves, but laws and programmes of this sort encourage our "higher" selves to realize our nobler and more generous ideals through social cooperation.[36]

CONCLUSION

Liberalism as an Ideology

What we can conclude, then, about liberalism as an ideology? Given the rift between welfare liberals and libertarians, or neoclassical liberals, does it even make sense to speak of liberalism as a single ideology? We think it does, although the division between the two camps is deep and may be widening. At present, however, their differences are largely matters of emphasis and disagreement about means, not ends. A quick look at how liberalism performs the four functions that all ideologies perform should make this point clear.

1. *Explanation* : First, all ideologies purport to explain why things are the way they are, with particular attention to social, economic, and political conditions. For liberals, these explanations are typically individualistic. Social conditions are the result of individual choices and actions. Liberals recognize that the choices open to individuals are often limited and frequently have consequences that no one intended or desired. Yet, despite the limits on their foresight and understanding, individuals still make choices that, taken together, explain why social conditions are as they are.[37]

2. *Evaluation :* When it comes to evaluating conditions, liberalism again turns to the individual. Conditions are good, as a rule, if the individual is free to do as he or she wishes without harming or violating the rights of others. The more freedom people have, liberals say the better the less freedom, the worse. And what freedom there is must be enjoyed as equally as possible. Thus, the liberal view of freedom requires that individuals have an equal opportunity to succeed. On this point all liberals agree. But they disagree, with welfare liberals going in one direction and libertarians

in another, on how best to provide equality of opportunity. For both, however, a society in which individuals enjoy an equal opportunity to choose freely is clearly better than one in which freedom is restricted and opportunity unequal.[38]

3. *Orientation :* Political ideologies also provide people with some sense of identity and orientation—of who they are and where and how they fit into the great scheme of things. Liberalism pictures people as rational individuals who have interests to pursue and choices to make. This is to say that liberals direct our attention to the characteristics that they believe all people share, not towards the differences that separate people from one another. Some liberals push this much further than others, and Bentham and the social Darwinists perhaps farthest of all, but there is a tendency among liberals to believe that deep down all women and men are fundamentally the same. Differences of culture, race, religion, gender, or nationality are ultimately superficial. Our identity is an individual—not a group—identity. At bottom, most people are rational, self-interested individuals who want to be free to choose how to live. Once we understand this, liberals believe, we will respect the right of others to live freely and expect them to respect our's in return.

4. *Programme :* As regards the programmatic function, liberals espouse programmes for promoting individual liberty and opportunity. Historically, this has meant that liberals have opposed religious conformity, ascribed status, economic privileges, political absolutism, and the tyranny of majority opinion. With these obstacles removes, individuals are free to worship (or not), as they see fit, to rise or fall in society according to their effort and ability, to compete on an equal footing in the market place, to exercise some control over government, and to think speak, and live in unconventional ways. On these points liberals seldom disagree. When some liberals began to say that freedom is not merely a matter of being left alone but a positive power

or ability to do what one chooses, disagreements emerged. Welfare liberals insist that the government must be enlisted in the struggle against illness, ignorance, prejudice, poverty and any other condition that threatens liberty and equality of opportunity, while neoclassical liberals complain that government "meddling" is itself the chief threat to liberty and equality.

Liberalism and the Democratic Ideal

At the end of the twentieth century, liberals are firmly committed to democracy but this has not always been the case. Througout most of its history, infact, liberalism has been more concerned with protecting people from their rulers than wish establishing rule by the people. From its beginning, as we have seen, liberalism has fought to remove those obstacles that stand in the way of the individuals freedom to live as he or she sees fit, and in the beginning most of those obstacles—religious conformity, ascribed status, political absolutism, monopolies, and other restraints on economic competition—were either provided or supported by government. Rather than strive to enable people to rule themselves through government, then the classical liberals struggled to free people from government. They tried, in other words, to reduce the areas of life that were considered public in order to expand the private sphere.

From the beginning, however, liberalism also displayed several democratic tendencies, the most notable being its premise of basic equality among human beings. Whether couched in terms of natural rights or the Utilitarians claim that everybody is to count for one and nobody for more than one, liberals have always argued from the premise that every person's rights or interests should count as much as everyone else's. Liberals opened the door for those who demanded that slavery be abolished and that women and the propertyless should be extended the right to vote, to run for public office, and generally be politically equal to property owning males.

This liberal tendency did not lead in an openly democratic direction until the 1800s, when Bentham and the Utilitarians began to argue that democracy gave every citizen the chance to protect his and later her interests. If the business of government is to promote the greatest good of the greatest number they reasoned, then the only way to determine the greatest good is to allow every citizen to say what is good for him or her. It was not until the 1800s that liberals began to regard the vote as a way to give everyone an equal chance to protect and promote his or her interest.[39]

For the most part, liberals favour democracy because it enables citizens to hold their government accountable, thereby protecting their personal interests. Some, including J.S. Mill, have gone further, arguing that democracy is good because it encourages wide spread political participation, which inturn enrichers people's lives by developing their intellectual and moral capacities. Yet, most liberals have attached no particular value to political activity, seeing it as simply one possible good among many. The state should be neutral, they say, leaving people free to pursue whatever they consider good as long as they respect other's freedom to do the same. If people find pleasure or satisfaction in public life, well and good, but if they derive more pleasure from private pursuits, then they should be free to follow that path.

As a rule, liberal democracy emphasizes the importance of individual rights and liberty. Everyone is supposed to be free to participate in public life, but the primary concern is to protect people from undue interference in their private affairs. Consequently, deciding what counts as "private" and how far an individuals "right to privacy" extends are matters of debate (as in the abortion controversy). For the liberal, democracy is good so long as it protects these rights and interests in privacy and free action. It does this primarily by making the government responsive to the needs and interests of the people, thus preventing arbitrary and tyrannical government. But if rule by the people begins to threaten the individual rights and liberties, then one can expect liberals to demand that it be curbed. In liberal democracy, in short, democracy is defined mainly in terms of the individual's right to be free from outside interference to do as he or she thinks best.[40]

REFERENCES

1. Thomas Hobbes, Leviathan, Chapter 11, see Terence Ball and Richard Dagger, eds., Ideals and Ideologies : A Reader, 3rd ed. (New York : Longman, 1999), Selection 11.
2. *Ibid.*, Chapter 13.
3. Conflict, consensus and confrontation are the natural part of the human life assumed liberalists.
4. John Locke, Second Treatise of Government, Paragraph 4; Ideals and Ideologies, Selection 12.
5. Liberty and equality are the important components of liberalism.
6. Thomas Jefferson, Political Writings (Cambridge University Press, 1998).
7. Locke's Political Theory, 14, (1986) : 263-289.
8. Ascribed status are those which are determined on the hereditary lines.
9. Muller, Freedom in the Western World, p. 382.
10. As translated in Thomas Paine, The Rights of Man (1792), see ideals and ideologies, selection 15.
11. Terence Ball, James Farr, and Russell L. Hanson, eds. (Cambridge University Press, 1989), pp. 211-219.
12. Adam Smith, The Wealth of Nations, Book I, Chapter II; see Ideals and Ideologies, selection 16.
13. In the medieval period serf and noble system prevailed Noble's exploited the serfs.
14. Thomas Hobbes, Above cited, *ibid.*, pp. 40-45.
15. Thomas Hobbes, *op. cited*, pp. 50-56.
16. John Locke, Treatises of Government, *op. cit.*, pp. 90-95.

17. Adam Smith, The Wealth of Nations, Book I, Chapter II. See Ideals and Ideologies, Selection 16.
18. Jeremy Bentham, Introduction to the Principles of Morals and Legislation (New York : Hafner, 1948), p. 1.
19. Jeremy Bentham *op. cit.,* pp. 20–25.
20. Over himself, over his own body and mind the individual is sovereign—John Stuart Mill, on Liberty.
21. J.S. Mill, *op. cit.,* pp. 70-75.
22. J.S. Mill, *op. cit.,* pp. 76-80.
23. J.S. Mill, *op. cit.,* pp. 82-85.
24. John Stuart Mill, on Liberty, Chapter I. See Ideals and Ideologies, Selection 18.
25. *Ibid.,* p. 114.
26. Ashcraft Richard, Revolutionary Politics and Locke's Two Treatises of Government, Princeton : Princeton University Press, 1986.
27. Elton, G.R., Reform Europe, 1517-1559, New York : Harper and Row, 1963.
28. Berlin, Isaiah, Four Essays on Liberty. Oxford : Oxford University Press, 1997.
29. William Graham Sumner, What Social Classes Owe to each other (Caldwell, ID : Caxton, 1970), p. 88. See Ideals and Ideologies, Selection 19.
30. Manning, D.J., Liberalism, New York : St Martin's Press, 1976.
31. *Op. cit., ibid.,* 70.
32. *Op. cit., ibid.,* 75.
33. Berlin, Isaiah, *ibid., op. cit.,* p. 78.
34. John Locke, *ibid., op. cit.,* p. 105.
35. John Locke, *ibid., op. cit.,* p. 108.
36. Thomas Hobbes, *ibid., op. cit.,* p. 125.
37. Thomas Hobbes, *ibid., op. cit.,* p. 150.
38. Adam Smith, *ibid., op. cit.,* p. 175.
39. Muller, *ibid., op. cit.,* p. 179.
40. Muller, *ibid., op. cit.,* p. 185.

9
FASCISM

Historians may well remember the twentieth century as the age of world wars, nuclear weapons, and a new kind of political regime—totalitarianism. All these developments are connected to political ideologies in one way or an other, but none more closely than totalitarianism. For totalitarianism is an attempt to take complete control of a society—not just its government, but all its social, cultural and economic institutions—in order to fulfil an ideological vision of how society ought to be organised and life ought to be lived.[1] Fascism is called as an ideology.

Infact, Mussolini and the Italian Fascists coined the word "totalitarian". They did this to define their revolutionary aims and to distinguish their ideology from liberalism and socialism, which they saw as advocates of democracy. Democracy requires equality of some sort, whether it be in the liberals insistence on equal opportunity for individuals or the socialists insistence on equal power for all in a classless society. Mussolini and his followers regarded these ideals with contempt, as Hitler and the Nazis. They did appeal to the masses for support, to be sure, but in their view the masses were to exercise power not by thinking, speaking, or voting for themselves, but by following their leaders to glory. As one of the Mussolini's many slogans put it—believe, obey, fight. Nothing more was asked nothing more was desired of the people. By embracing totalitarianism, then fascists also rejected democracy.[2]

In this respect, fascism is a reactionary ideology. It took shape in the years following World War I as a reaction against the two leading ideologies of the time, liberalism and socialism. Unhappy and the liberal emphasis on the individual and the socialist emphasis on contending social classes, the fascists provided a view of the world in which individuals and classes were to be absorbed into at all-embracing whole a mighty empire under the control of a single party and a supreme leader. Like the Reactionaries of the early 1800s, they also rejected the faith in reason that they thought formed the foundation for liberalism and socialism alike. Reason is less reliable, both Hitler and Mussolini declared, than intuitions and emotions—what we sometimes call "gut instincts".

To say that fascism is in some ways a reactionary ideology is not to say, however, that fascists are simply reactionaries or extreme conservatives. In many ways, they are quite different. Many fascists have been openly hostile to religion and a few of them have had any respect for hereditary monarchs and aristocrats. Fascism in its most distinctive forms has been openly revolutionary, eager not only to change society, but to change it dramatically. This by itself sets fascists apart from conservatives, who cannot abide rapid and radical change. So, too, does the fascist plan to concentrate power in the hands of a totalitarian state led by a single party and a supreme leader. Fascist vision is to a unified state bending to the will of a single-all-powerful leader.[3]

Fascism, then, is neither conservative nor simply reactionary. It is, as the original fascists boasted, a new and distinctive ideology.

Fascism : The Background

Although fascism did not emerge as a political ideology until the 1920s, its roots reach back over a century to the reaction against the intellectual and cultural movement that dominated European thought in the eighteenth century—the Enlightenment. The thinkers of the Enlightenment dreamed a dream of reason. Taking the scientific discoveries of the seventeenth and eighteenth centuries as their model and inspiration, the Enlightenment Philosophers claimed that the application of reason could remove all the social and political evils that stood in the way of happiness and progress. Reason can light the minds of men and women, they proclaimed, freeing them from ignorance, error and superstition.[4] The two great political currents that flow from the enlightenment are liberalism and socialism. Different as they are in other respects, these two ideologies are alike in sharing the premises of the Enlightenment. These premises include.

1. Humanism

The idea that human beings are the source and measure of value, with human life valuable in and of itself. As Kant (1724-1804) put it, human beings belong to the "kingdom of ends". Each person is an end-in-himself in Kant Words, not something that others may use, like a tool, as a means of accomplishing their own selfish ends.

2. Rationalism

The idea that humanbeings are rational creatures and that human reason, epitomized in scientific inquiry, can solve all mysteries and reveal solutions to all the problems that men and women face.

3. Secularism

The idea that religion may be a source of comfort and insight, but not of absolute and unquestionable truths for guiding public life. The Enlightenment thinkers different from one another in their religious views. Some like John Locke and Kant, remained Christians, others like Voltaire (1694-1778), rejected Christianity but believed in a God who had created a world as well—ordered as a watch, which the "divine watch maker" had wound and left to run, still others were atheists. But even those who took their Christianity seriously regarded religion as something to be confined largely to private life, and therefore out of place in politics. The irreligious among the Enlightenment philosophers simply dismissed religion as an outmoded superstition that must give way to rational and scientific ideas.[5]

4. Progressivism

The idea that human history is the story of progress, or improvement—perhaps even inevitable improvement—in the human condition. Once the shakes of ignorance and superstition have been broken, human reason will be free to order society in a rational way, and life will steadily and rapidly become better for all.

5. Universalism

The idea that there is a single, universal, human nature that binds all human beings together, despite differences of race, culture, or religious creed. Human beings are all equal members of Kant's "kingdom of ends"–who share the same essential nature, including pre-eminently the capacity for reason.

These Enlightenment views are often linked to liberalism but they provided much of the inspiration for socialism as well. Indeed, modern socialism arose in part from the complaint that liberalism was not going far enough in its attempt to remake society in the image of enlightenment ideals.[6] Fascism, however, grows out of the very different conviction that the ideals of the enlightenment are not worth-pursuing a claim first put forward in the late eighteenth and early nineteenth centuries.

The term fascism is derived from the latin word Fasces, which means bundle. In ancient Rome, the faces (a bundle of rods tied around an ax) symbolished political authority supported by the unification of the nation.[7] Fascism first of all arouse in Italy under the leadership of Benito Mussoli. Mussolini shouted typically belligerent manner, "Action, Deeds—These alone matter. Leave theory to the scribblers".

Mass rallies, Waving banners, beating drums, blaring horns, repeated slogans, uniforms and decorations, precision marching and physical presence of the leader. Violence in the pursuit of power.

Main Objectives and General Principles of Fascism

Fascists disregard for any set of political philosophy or principles. For them, formal principles are iron and tin fetters. According to Mussoli, Italy needed not programmes but men and will power. The fascist movement came first and its philosophy afterwards. The fascist principles are to be found not in formal treatises, but in deeds and proposals of men actively engaged in realising the fascist aims. The fascist theory was merely a guide to action. The doctrine was simply to serve the requirements of the main objectives of the fascists. The fascist aims were both constructive and comprehensive.[8]

Mussolini said, my objective is simple. "I want to make Italy great, respected and feared." I want to make a greater prosperity always possible for the whole people. I want to create a political organisation to express, to guarantee and to safeguard our development. For the achievement of this objective, they followed ail types of methods, tactics and doctrines howsoever inconsistent they might me.

The fascist stood for politics alone. Their ideas, tactics, plans, everything depended upon the ever-changing decisions of their leader. Mussolini who was the real embodiment of all power. The people were to obey the leader blindly and carryout his orders without any complaint. They made their leaders as the embodiment of state power who could do not wrong. Man was completely subordinated to the requirements of all Almighty state. Mussolini himself said, "no need for dogma, discipline suffices."[9]

OBJECTIVE AND GENERAL PRINCIPLES

1. The Fascist Idea of the Nation

Fascism, conceives of the nation as the ultimate moral being. It is not merely an aggregate of individuals, but an organisation evolving through countless generations. The fascist equate nation with society. Thus, the nation according to fascists represents the ultimate synthesis of all the material and spiritual values. Individual and group interests must be subordinated to the interests of the nation which alone is the 'march of God on earth' and which alone can change class conflicts into national co-operation. All things and persons are subordinate to the nation and it is through the nation alone that they can realise themselves. Glorification of the nation-state is the first chief objective of the fascists. "Men owe duties to the nation and the nation owes duties to none". A nation knows no superiors and its seeks self-expression and expansion. According to fascists, a nation has got the right to exist only if it can successfully compete with other nations in the general struggle for existence. The fascist nationalism is imperialist in character. They say, imperialism is the external, and immutable law of life. The fascists stand for the absolute sovereignty, moral and legal of the national state. It's interests are the interests of the people and in case of conflict the interests of the nation must have precedence over the interests of the living citizens. For the active and efficacious participation in the national life, it is necessary for the people to be guided by the fascist slogans of 'Responsibility, Discipline and Hierarchy' than by democratic slogans of 'Liberty Equality and Fraternity". The very idea that the nation is superior to all its members or any of its groups and that its interests are superior to individual or group interests is the determining factor of the fascist principles of governmental structure and policy. For this very reason, fascist conception of authority is autocratic and aristocratic which was to represent not individuals but groups and which was to be centralised one.[10]

For fascists, the nation was the supreme arbiter of the people and it was their duty to serve the nation faithfully, honestly and ardently. Only those actions, thoughts and sentiments of the people were to be considered good which contributed to the growth and enrichment of the power of the nation. They used all the means of propaganda for inculcating love for the nation in the hearts of the people. Nation was the supreme entity. It's glorification was the end to be achieved. All things and beings were to be used for the attainment of this objective.

2. The Fascist's Idea of the State and the Individual

The state is all powerful controlling and directing the lives of citizens. The fascist state, of course, is totalitarian in nature. It believes that it has both the moral and legal right to control and regulate every act and interest of the individual and groups of individuals, if in the judgement of the state, such control is necessary. Politics, economics, art, literature, education and religion all are to be serve the needs of the state. The so-called individual rights are simple non-sense. The individuals have simply duties towards the state. The state represents the ideal unity of its members. So, every individual must realise himself within the state and he must put himself completely at the disposal of the state. Duty discipline and sacrifice are demanded from the individuals. According to fascist creed-state is an organic whole. The fascist state must be all powerful, totalitarian and authoritarian. No organisation can remain outside the state. Fascism is therefore, near the people. It has educated them politically and morally and has organised them not only from the professional and economic point of view, but also from the military, cultural, educational, recreative point of view. Rocco said, fascist state interprets, develops and potentiates the whole life of the people. No individuals or groups (political parties, cultural associations, economic unions, social classes) exist outside the state. The fascist state was not only totalitarian. It was also authoritarian. According to them sovereignty rests not with the people, but with the state itself. Fascism reflects the dogma of popular sovereignty and substitute for it that of state sovereignty. It is in the king (in name) or in the Mussolini, as head of the government (in reality) that the sovereign power is embodied.[11]

The individual is what he is, because of his being in the state. The fascist state is sovereign and the government is authoritarian. There is complete identification between the individual and the state. There is perfect synthesis of the community and the individual in the state. But no such things as inalienable individual rights exist in a fascist state.

3. Liberty Under Fascist State

Under fascism, liberty is an out moded ideal. They put more emphasis on the might of the state than on the liberty of the individuals. Their contention was that liberty of the people depended upon the strength of the nation. According to them, Italy needed law, order and efficiency rather than liberty.[12] For them, real liberty was possible only under a political system which rigidly enforced law, order and efficiency. Liberty was not a natural endowment of the Nature, it was simply a concession made by the state. Real liberty consisted not in doing something freely but in subjection to law. Liberty consisted not a right but a duty. According to fascists writes Coker 'law and state' are the supreme manifestations of liberty. The citizen gains true personality and freedom not by safeguarding some private interest, but only by losing or merging himself in larger units—his family, church and finally state. Fascism forces the individual to develop his personality on behalf of the nation. Thus, in the fascist state an individual was free only if he completely identified himself with the will of the people, and the will of the people was the will of the state. The state was the sole judge of the nature and extent of freedom to be enjoyed by the people. Individual develops his personality and freedom on behalf of the state.

Thus, we find that the fascist conception of liberty is totally different from the democratic conception. For democrats the claims of the individuals for freedom of thought, speech, association and faith are essential for the development of one's personality. These freedoms build the individuality and personality of a man. But to fascists the idea of development of the personality of an individual is simple nonsense. According to them the state being an ethical whole, there is no place for independent existence for man apart from the state. Whatever the freedom is enjoyed by the individual is within the state and within the limits imposed by the state.

4. Fascist Repudiation of Democracy and Liberalism

The fascists were the enemies of both democracy and liberalism. They had no faith in parliamentary form of government. The fascists described democracy as stupid, corrupt, slow-moving, visionary, impracticable and inefficient. They compared it with a decaying corpse. For fascists, parliaments were 'taking shops' and the country needed action and not talk.[13]

5. Fascist Repudiation of Socialist Ideas

The fascists were anti-socialists and anti-communists. They rejected the socialist, doctrine of economic determination. They believed that materialism was not everything. Religion and patriotism also played a vital role in the lives of the people. Then the fascists did not believe in the theory of class-struggle. They wanted all classes to co-operate for the glorification of the state. They thought that class struggle was not natural and inevitable. They refused to believe that all history was history of class struggle. A country like Italy needs not class antagonism but class-co-operation. According to them, the state was not only aimed to abolish struggle but also to find out the causes responsible for the origin and growth of class conflicts and then to remove them.

Fascism was not the protector of any class whatsoever, but a supreme regulator of the relations between all citizens of a state. It aimed to bring together both the employees and the employers and make them work co-operatively for the glorification of the nation. The fascists rejected the idea that human happiness laid in economic well beings. According to Mussolini, the idea of economic well-being alone would reduce man to the level of animals caring for the thing only to be fat and well-fed and would degrade humanity to a purely physical existence. Anti-patriotic attitude of the socialists was another reason for fascists hostility to words socialism.

Thus, we see that fascism rejected almost all the basic principles of socialism—materialistic doctrine of surplus value and its internationalism. It believed simply in holiness and in heroism, in actions not influenced by economic motive, direct or indirect.[14]

6. Fascism and Education

Building up of the character and inculcation of the national tradition was the primary aim of fascists education. University professors are required to swear to maintain their loyalty to the fascist regime and to inculcate the fascist ideals in the minds of their students. The prescribed text books of the schools direct attention to the beauty and grandeur of Italy, the glory of her historic achievements in literature, art, music, industry, commerce and war, and the validity record of the fascists under Mussolini's skillful and heroic leadership in delivering Italy from Bolshevism. Thus, there was complete control of education and educational institutions by the fascist government.[15]

7. Fascism, War and Internationalism

Instead of peace, they advocated war and raise the war slogan to the level of an ideal. The fascism is an enemy to internationalism. International peace is according to them, a cowards dream. For Mussolini "at bottom internationalism is an absurd fable." The fascists, therefore, advocated nationalism as opposed to internationalism and they glorified was as opposed to peace.

Mussolini and Italian Fascism

Benito Mussolini was born in a village in rural Italy in 1883 the year that Karl Marx died. Mussolini's father was a blacksmith and an atheist, his mother a school teacher and a Catholic. As a young man, Mussolini himself was a school teacher, but he soon took up political journalism and Marxist Socialism. In 1912, he became editor Avanti (Forward), the largest of Italy's Socialist Journals. As editor he remained a revolutionary socialist, proclaiming that capitalism would fall only after a violent proletarian uprising. Even at this point, however, Mussolini placed more emphasis on the will to engage in revolutionary struggle than on economic factors and contradictions of capitalism.[16]

Benito Mussolini (1883-1945)

To Mussolini, "War is to the male what child-bearing is to the female" true freedom, in the fascist view, is found in serving the state, and there is nothing more fulfilling than doing one's part, however small, to promote its glory. But how was the glory of the state to be achieved? Through military conquest, Mussolini said, and conquest required the discipline and loyalty of the Italian people. This Mussolini and the fascists attempted to win through massive propaganda efforts, always designed to appeal to the emotions and instincts of the people. The people were a mass, a "herd" incapable of leading themselves.

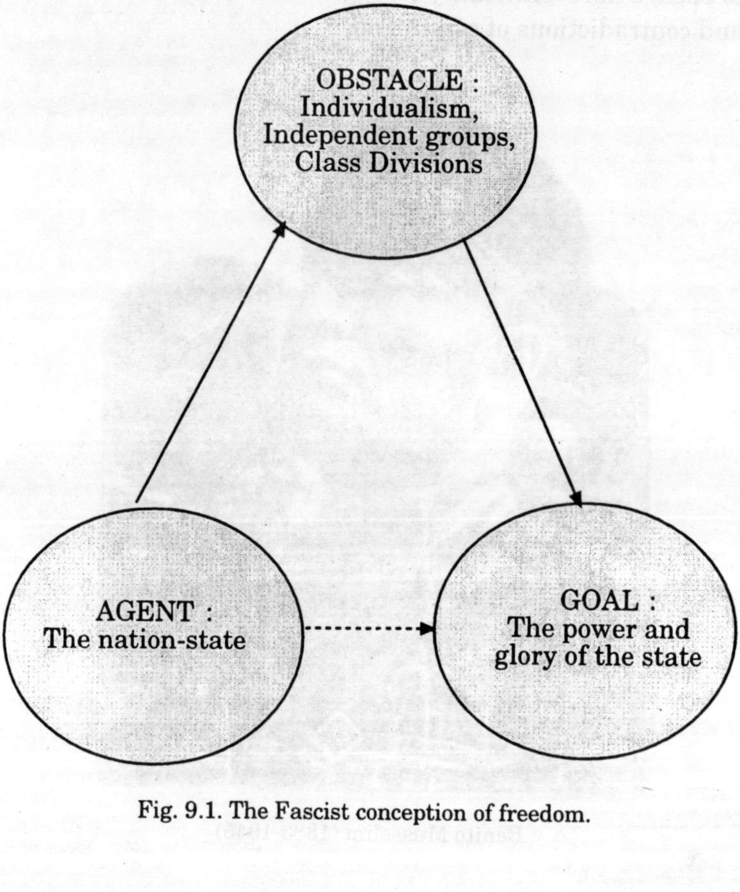

Fig. 9.1. The Fascist conception of freedom.

They needed an elite to guide them, and they especially needed a dictator with an almost mystical ability to know where their true interests lay. Hence, the people were told, in schools and in speeches and in slogans emblazoned on walls, that "Mussolini is always right," Everything newspapers, radio, schools was to be used to instill this conviction in the people.

NAZISM IN GERMANY

Hitler and Nazism

Just as Italian fascism was closely associated with Benito Mussolini, so its German counterpart, Nazism, was inextricably linked with Adolf Hitler. Hitler was born in Austria, near the German border, in 1889. Moving to Vienna when he was 18, Hitler tried, unsuccessfully, to establish himself as an artist.[17] He remained there for several years, living practically as a vagrant, until World War I began. Hitler then joined the German Army and served with distinction, twice winning the Iron Cross for bravery. He was in the hospital when the war ended in 1918, and shortly thereafter his political career began.

When Germany surrounded to end World War I, German troops were still on French soil, and many Germans believed that surrender was unnecessary. Germany had not been defeated on the battle field, they charged, but betrayed by traitorous politicians. Hitler shared these sentiments. After his release from the hospital, Hitler remained with the army as a spy. In this role he attended the meetings in Munich of a tiny group that called itself the German Worker's Party. Somehow, Hitler saw an opportunity in this group, which he joined in 1920. He soon became the leader of the party under its new name, the National Socialist German Worker's Party—or Nazis as they were called from the abbreviation of the first two words.

Adolf Hitler (1889-1945)

The party grew quickly under Hitler's direction. Hitler established a paramilitary organisation. This is an attempt to over how the government for which Hitler was arrested and tried for treason. Hitler received five year prison sentence and served only nine months of it. During his imprisonment, he wrote the first part of his autobiography, Mein Kampf, or My Battle. In that book Hitler made clear the basic outlines of his ideology. Like the Italian fascists slogan, "War is to the male what child bearing is to the famle," Hitler's words also reveal the fascist pre-occupation with masculinity, which the Nazis and fascists associated with strength, action and dominance.

In most respects, Nazism in Germany closely resembled fascism in Italy. There was the same hatred of liberalism and communism, for instance, the same attitude toward the masses, who were to be molded to the will of the great leader through propaganda and indoctrination, the same reliance on an organic conception of society, the same appeal to military might and the need for discipline and sacrifice, the same emphasis on nationalism, and the same totalitarian spirit. Neither Hitler nor Mussolini had much interest in the economic matters, moreover, at least not as long as they thought that their countries were producing enough weapons and other war material.[18]

From the beginning Nazism relied, and continues to rely, on the idea that race is the fundamental characteristic of human beings. Fascism was not, and need not be, a racist ideology, in other words, Nazism was and is. Indeed, racial theory is at the core of Nazism. So much so that we can define Nazism in terms of the simple formula, fascism + racism = Nazism. This belief is especially clear in the Nazi views of human nature and freedom. For Hitler and his followers, the fundamental fact of human life is that human beings belong to different races. There is no such thing as a universal human nature, in their view, because of the differences that distinguish one race from another mark each race for a different role or destiny in the world. Hitler claimed that the Aryans were an extraordinary race, superior one, the fountain of most of what was civilized and worthwhile in the world. On the basis of the speculation, the Nazis decided that it was the destiny of Aryans to rule others, to subjugate the inferior races so that culture could advance and reach new and glorious heights.

The Nazis also drew upon this racial view of human nature in developing their conception of freedom. Like the Italian fascists, they opposed the liberal view that freedom is a matter of individual liberty. But the Nazis gave this their characteristic racial twist. The only freedom that counts, they said, is the freedom of the Volk (nation) who belong to the "master race". Freedom should be the freedom of Aryans because that is nature's plan. But there are obstacles in the way of the Aryan race's realising its destiny. There is the obstacle, first, of the "inferior" races who are doing what they can to drag the Aryans down to their own level. And there is also the obstacle presented by certain ideas and ideals specifically—the humanist ideas of the Enlightenment.[19] These were "Jewish ideal" according to Hitler, ideas that made even Aryans soft and squeamish. Because these ideas of universal brotherhood and equality are embedded in liberalism and Marxism, it followed for Hitler that these ideologies are not merely obstacles, but enemies to be rooted out and destroyed. Every individual, in the Nazi's view, is merely a cell in the larger organism. The destiny of the organism is also the individuals destiny.

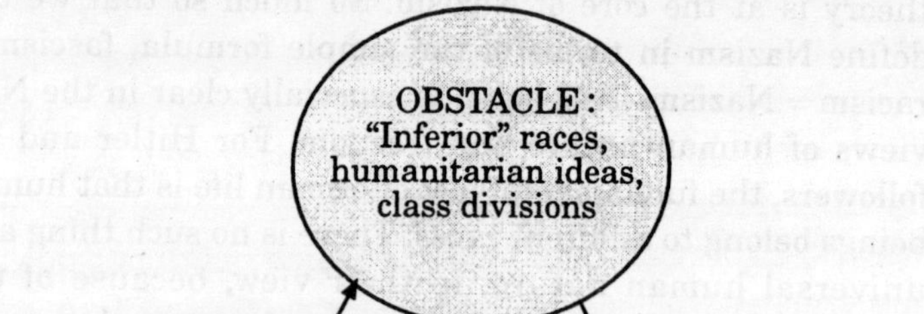

Fig. 9.2. The Nazi conception of freedom.

THE BASIC IDEAS OF THE NAZISM

1. On the Nature and Functions of the State

For the Nazi's the state should not only be obeyed but worshipped. It was a true state. The nation state must have supreme and absolute power over all its citizens. The individual has no meaning for the Nazis. It had no separate existence apart from the state. It must always be subordinated and sacrificed for the community the nation and the nation-state. Common interest before self-interest or the welfare of the community was more important than the welfare of the individual were their common slogans. The individual was to have no freedom or initiate. He was to find his happiness in the obedience to the orders of the state. He was simply to serve the needs and requirements of the state. His welfare had no meaning before the welfare of the nation state *i.e.,* the whole. Thus, an individual could find himself only in the state. It was service of the state which constituted his freedom. With the dictum of Kant and Fichte that the individual possesses not rights but duties, they ardently agreed. One of their axioms was that true freedom for the individual consists of subordinating himself to the Volk (nation-state) and working for its welfare. Thus, the Nazis followed no sphere of privacy to any one.[20]

Nazis controlled every sphere of human life—religion, education, art, literature, music, science, recreation, drama, theatre and economic matters and even fashions. Their state was completely authoritarian, absolute in all respects. The surprising thing was that the Nazis thought and the German's believe that their true freedom consisted in their total subordination to the nation and it was by this action alone that he become truly and really free. They followed the fascist slogan—"everything is within the state and for the state, nothing is outside the state and against the state."

2. Nazi's Criticism of Democracy

The Nazi's were violent in their attacks upon any and every form of democratic or parliamentary government. Hitler thought that it was democracy which brought ruin of Germany. He wrote "At all times it has been the principles of democracy which have brought people to ruin." According to Nazis, democracy was the greatest of all falacies. What men needed and what they really wanted, was to led and governed by the few who had the necessary understanding and ability to think and act. Like fascists, they supported the doctrine of government by the political elite which according to them was in perfect harmony with the nature of man. They had very poor opinion about the human beings. According to Hitler democracy directly led to Bolshevism. They attacked democracy from different points of view. In a democracy, they held the real authority rested not with the elected representatives of the people, but a few wire-pullers who worked behind the scenes. The foolish many should be controlled by the wise few and the wise few inturn must be guided by a single leader. The leader must have absolute and unlimited power to make or unmake any law whatsoever and to appoint and dismiss all officials of the government. This single leader must be supreme over all the branches of government—executive, legislative and judicial.[21]

Thus, we see that Nazis of Germany like their fascist friends of Italy were thoroughly anti-democratic and anti-liberal. Being against democracy, the Nazis were equally critical of such doctrines—as the theory of separation of powers and theory of check and balances. They have mentally denied that government rested upon the consent of the governed.

3. Nazis Attack on Communism

They insisted that property could only be acquired and held subject to certain definite conditions and it was for the state to laydown those conditions. According to the Nazis, it was the duty of the state to provide employment and subsistence to all able bodied persons and this could be done only if the state is supervised and regulated all possible forms of economic activities. The Nazi's movement was a middle-class movement.

4. Nazi's Control of Economic Life

The Nazi's aimed to establish full political control over the economic forces and economic activities inside Germany. Membership in the state was compulsory. The state had complete control over the currency, credit and credit expansion. Through the national economic chamber the state could interfere directly in the affairs of any industrial, commercial coercion. Even inside the individual firm the state has the power to prescribe types, quantity and quality of production. The owners of a business could be removed by the government for anti-social conduct or any such thing. The labour front was the biggest estate. The Nazi ideology did not accept the view that, there was conflict between labour and the capital. According to it, both the ampler and the workers were to work together for furthering the purposes of the enterprise and for the benefit of the nation and the state in general. Both strikes and lockouts were prohibited. All the disputes were to be by the labour trustee. Further, in Germany, class distinctions were totally wiped out. The food estates included both the landlords tenants, farmers and agricultural workers. Similarly, the labour front included both the owners of the factories, executive officers and the skilled and unskilled workers. Those, the German system was more authoritarian and totalitarian than the Italian. Thus, Nazis had complete control over the economic life of the nation.

5. The Nazi's Belief in the Use of Force

The Nazi's believed in the use of brute force for the achievements of its objectives and for meeting every type of opposition. "Might is right" was their principle. Hitler was of the view that force to be successful must be used ruthlessly and persistently. Their philosophy was a matter of fact 'the philosophy of sword'. As Hitler said, "he how would live must fight." He who does not wish to fight in this world has not the right to exist. Such a saying may sound harsh, but that is how the matter stands. They used force not only in their internal matters with the aim to establish authoritarian and totalitarian dictatorship, they used it in the external field also for establishing the supremacy of the German nation. War was considered to be the climax of human achievement, the father of all thing and the most simple affirmation of life. Thus, the Nazi's could be described as brutalism in its most naked form.[22]

6. Nazis Role of Propaganda

The Nazis were not only great organisers, they were great propagandists also. Children, young men and women, industrialists and laboures were all organised into Nazi propaganda. The pulpit, the stage, the cinema, the radio, the press 'art' science, literature and school were all made instruments of Nazi propaganda. Hitler himself was the master in the art of propaganda. According to him, it is to the masses that propaganda must be addressed. It must not aim at instruction. It must work always and wholly on the emotions. The presentation may be infinately varied, but the theme must be always the same. The Nazis held the view that propaganda cold persuade people to believe that Heaven is Hell. According to Hitler propaganda had nothing to do with abstract truth. He believed in the doctrine of big lie. By telling big-lies he made the German people follow him blindly.[23]

7. Anti-Jewish Policy of the Nazis

The Nazis believed that the German armies were never defeated in the battle field. They were stabbed in the back by the Jewish-Marxist traitors. They thought they were in league with Marxists. They regarded the Jew as greatest misfortune of the German nation. So, all the Jews must be exterminated from earth. Following this policy millions of Jews were but cheered to death, thrown into concentration camps and gas chambers.

8. Nazi's on the Role of Religion and Women

All the Nazis were anti-catholic, anti-Protestant. The high priest of the new German paganism is Hitler himself. He is the real Holy Ghost. Hitler is lonely. So is God. Hitler is like a God. Hitler is a new, a greater and a more powerful Jesus Christ.

As regards women, the Nazis held the conventional views. According to them the sole end for which women were meant was to produce children and sending them to war. Papen said "Mothers must exhaust themselves in order to give life to children". Fathers must fight on the battle field in order to secure the future of their sons. According to the Declaration of the women's order of the Red Swastika, there is no higher or finer privilege for a women than that of sending her children to war. In female education emphasis was laid on motherhood. Large families were encouraged by giving a number of tax concessions for increasing the German race. Birth control was considered as a sin. Home was regarded as the natural and proper place for women.

9. Nazis on Imperialism

The Nazis followed a policy of expansion and conquest, and thus, they were thoroughly imperialists in their outtook and designs. Germany must have cultivable lands for her expanding population and they were justified in seizing new territories. Hitler said, "We are not the police protectors of poor little nations, but the soldiers of our own." The world was not made for coward peoples. Hitler aimed to make Germany militarily strong enough so as to enable him not only to get back Germany's stolen colonies, but also more and for millions. Thus, Nazis were thoroughly imperialists who believed in the doctrine that right laid in strength alone.[24]

10. Nazi on Internationalism

The Nazis were patriots par-excellence. They loved their fatherland more than anything else. Glorification of greater Germany was the ultimate aim. They were enemies of internationalism which was an absurd doctrine for them. They believed in the supremacy of the nation-state only. They looked upon international peace as a coward's dream. Their belief in socialism, use of force for settling disputes and glorification of internationalism. Germany under Hitler withdrew from the League of Nations as it could not subscribe to the doctrine of settling of differences by negotiation and peaceful methods. For them, force and war were the only vehicles for resolving differences. A nation could progress only by coming into conflict with other nations and showing thereby its strength and supremacy. Thus, the Nazi's had utmost hatred for any kind of international amity an co-operation.[25]

11. Nazi's Doctrine of Racial Supremacy

According to Maxey "the most prominent feature of Nazi philosophy was its emphasis on race and its insistence that race is the measure of all things." The Nazis were not only gave whole-hearted support to the doctrines of social Darwinism, they were equally enthusiastic in their support of the eugenic creed which was closely related to social Darwinism. The basic principles of this creed are :

1. Men are naturally and innately unequal,
2. These innate differences are hereditary,
3. The innately superior persons and stocks show a tendency to rise to the top of the social ladder,
4. The state must take steps to secure the preservation of the superior stocks.

The Nazi leaders accepted all these premises without any reservation. They rather elaborated, amplified and propagated them. The ground had already been prepared in

Germany by the teachings of Chamber Laine who developed the doctrine of race superiority. It was also generally believed that the White race was superior to all others, that the teutons were the best of the white race, and the Germans the best of the teutons.

The Nazis added practically nothing to these already existing racial doctrines. They simply made them more refined and more acceptable to the people of Germany. The converted the doctrine of radicalism into a kind of myth which could mobilise the German Youth. For the Nazis the inequalities were the result of hereditary. They were eager to create a new aristocracy of the finest stock in the country. They aimed to protect the superior stocks with the help of the state.

The Nazi raised the race doctrine to mystical heights. According to Hitler 'all that is not race in this world is trash'. For Rosenberg, the idea of genuine natural state was born out of the concept of race. As certain family stocks were superior to other family stocks, so were certain races innately and externally superior to the other races. They accepted the view that each race had not only its physical characteristics, but also certain mental, emotional and spiritual traits which were peculiar to itself. According to Rosenberg, each race had a soil of its own and each must find its soul through the recognition of its own supreme value. The Nazi's put lot of emphasis on the purity of race.[26]

After surveying the races of the world Hitler came to the conclusion that the Aryan race was really the most important and the superior one of all the races and the purist—Aryan Stock was to be found in Germany alone. The Aryan was regarded as the highest image of God. According to Hitler, all the products of civilization, art, science, and technique were the creative product of the Aryan and an Aryan was always ready to place all his gifts and powers at the service of the community. He was willing to sacrifice himself for the good of the whole, to laydown his life if need be for the preservation of his species. Thus, the human civilization and culture were bound up with the existence of the Aryan. According to Hitler, almost all the nations of the world were mixture of blood. It was only Germany that possessed a large store of unmixed North-German Stocks the Aryans. The new German state must undertake the task of assembling and preserving the most valuable racial elements and must raise them to a position of domination. Hitler laid utmost stress on purity of race. He believed that races were higher and lower, stronger and weaker.[27]

These racial doctrines provided Hitler with many excuses to follow his policy of totalitarianism and authoritarianism. The Nazis took steps even by legislation to increase the stock of pure Aryan race. They aimed to build strong German race which could be able to win the world.

12. The Nazi Party and the Principle of Leadership

Germany under Hitler developed one party system. The Nazi party was the only party in the country. It was the embodiment of the philosophy of National Socialism. It was the connecting link between the volk or the community and the state. It was this party which brought all the Germans under the common leadership. There is a complete identification between the party and the state. The party dominated every aspect of life of the people. Only the leading members of the party were appointed to the high as well as low posts in the country. The labour was completely controlled by it. As a matter of fact, the labour front which had complete sweep over the economic life of the people was practically a Nazi organisation. Storm troopers and the black guards were its militant wings which were always ready to carry out its orders and crush every type of opposition with force. It organised the youths of the country under its youth organisation. It was opposed to every type of democratic thinking and working. It was all authoritarian.

According to Barker, leadership is so prominent factor,

that it is called the core not only of the constitution of the party but also of its doctrine. Leader was the essential title of the head of the state. Acting on the ideas, the Nazi's advocated the hierarchical system of the party and the government working not from bottom upwards, but from the top towards the bottom. They had no faith in democratic leadership which emerged from the bottom. They on the other hand, believed in the leadership of one man. Heroes are born from time to time and it is upon these that all depends. Such a hero was Hitler who was raised to the mystical heights by the Nazi Party. His word was law. He was a God. He was at once the head of the state, the government, the nation and the army. He was infact, everything. He is an offshoot of the folk—said Sabine. He is the genius or the hero conceived as a man of pure race. All the Nazi's believed that the state must be run by the aristocracy and the aristocracy must be headed by an all powerful leader.[28]

Such a leader was Hitler who held all the legislative, executive and judicial powers in his own hands. The leader was the superman who must control entire life of the nation and thereby make it supreme. The Nazi Party aimed to replaced parliamentary government by the elite headed by a leader who was the superman. According to them, a majority was nothing but stupidity personified. The majority principle was to be substituted by personality. A majority was never able to think and organise. It was only an individual who could do so. The Nazi's believed that blood and iron were more effective and potent weapons for enforcing policy than speeches and majorities. The Nazi party was a party of disciplined members as Hitler believed that the strength of the party laid in discipline obedience.[29]

CONCLUSION

Fascism and Nazism as an Ideology

One feature of these two 'Isms' is clear. No matter what the form, these two 'Isms' *i.e.,* Fascism and Nazism have always tried to win mass support by appealing to people in the simplest, most emotional terms. This becomes evident as we look at how Fascism and Nazism perform the four functions of a political ideology.

1. Explanation. Why are social conditions the way they are? Fascists typically answer this question with some account of heroes and villains. Usually they concentrate on the scoundrels or traitors who conspire to keep the nation or volk weak in order to serve their own personal interests. They look for scapegoats, in other words, and blame all problem on them.

2. Evaluation. Whether a situation is good or bad, according to them, will usually depend on some evaluation of a nation's or volk's unity and strength. If the people are fragmented, at odds with one another, then it is time to hunt down the villains who are tearing the volk or nation apart. If the people are united behind their party and their leader, on the other hand, then all is well.

3. Orientation. What is one's place in the world, one's primary source of belonging or identification? According to the Italian fascists, it is the nation, to the Nazis, the nation defined in racial terms. In either case, the individual should recognize that he or she is of no significance as an individual, but only as a member of the organic whole—the nation-state or the race–that gives meaning and purpose to his or her life.

4. Programme. What is to be done? Again, the answer is simple—believe, obey, fight. Follow one's leaders in the struggle against the enemies of the nation or race, and do whatever is necessary to bring glory to one's people by helping to establish it as a leading power in the world. Give everything to the state, keep nothing from the state, and do nothing against the state.

Fascism and the Democratic Ideal

In its strongest forms, then, whether it be Italian fascism, German Nazism, or neo-Nazism, Fascism and Nazism are the totalitarian ideologies. Of all the political ideologies, it is the only one to reject democracy altogether. It does respond to the democratic ideal, to be sure, but it responds with contempt. For the Fascist and Nazism, democracy is merely another name for division and weakness in a world where unity and strength are what truly matter.[30]

REFERENCES

1. McGovern, W.M., From Luther to Hitler, p. 531.
2. Ebenstein, W., Today's Isms, Third ed., 95.
3. Barnes, J.S., The Universal Aspects of Fascism, p. 35.
4. J.S. Roucek and others, Introduction to Political Science (1954), p. 90.
5. Maxey, Political Philosophies, pp. 638-39.
6. Coker, F.W., Recent Political Thought, p. 460.
7. *Ibid.*, p. 461.
8. Coker, *op. cit.*, pp. 461-62.
9. Mussolini, My Autobiography: Translated by Richard Washburn Child, Hutchinson and Co., London, p. 59.
10. *Ibid.*, p. 66.
11. Schneider, H.W., Making the Fascist State, p. 56.
12. McGovern, W.M., *op. cit.*, pp. 533-34.
13. *Ibid.*, p. 534.
14. Mussolini, Benito, My Autobiography, p. 103.
15. Mussolini, Benito, *op. cit.*, p. 171.
16. Quoted in H. Finer, Mussolini's Italy (New York, 1935), pp. 17-18.
17. Maxey, *op. cit.*, p. 638.
18. McGovern, *op. cit.*, p. 538.

19. Maxey, *op. cit.*, p. 618.
20. Quoted in Schneider, Making the Fascist State, p. 276.
21. *Ibid.*, pp. 274-75.
22. Hans Kohn, Nationalism : Its Meaning and History, (Princeton, NJ : D. Van Nostrand, 1955), p. 36.
23. Quoted in A. James Gregor, Contemporary Political Ideologies (New York : Random House, 1968), p. 131.
24. Adolf Hitler, Mein Kampf, Trans., Ralph Manheim (Boston : Houghton Mifflin, 1943), p. 42. Also in Ideals and Ideologies, Selection 48.
25. Quoted in Gregor, Contemporary Radical Ideologies, p. 197.
26. Quoted in Raymond E. Murphy, *et. al*; "National Socialism" in Readings on Fascism and National Socialism (Chicago Swallow Press, 1952), p. 65.
27. Quoted in Leonard Thompson, The Political Mythology of Apartheid (New Haven : Yale University Press, 1985), p. 29.
28. Griffin, Roger, The Nature of Fascism, London : Routledge, 1993.
29. Laqueur, Walter, Fascism : Past, Present, Future, New York, Oxford University Press, 1996, pp. 40-45.
30. Laqueur, Walter, *op. cit.*, 1997, pp. 70-75.

GLOSSARY OF POLITICAL THINKERS

This glossary provides brief biographical details about the major political theorists discussed in the text.

1. **Bentham Jeremy (1748-1832).** British philosopher, economist and legal theorist, the principal exponent of Utilitarianism.
2. **Burke Edmund (1729-1797).** Dublin-born, British statesman and political theorist. Reflections on the Revolution in France (1790) established him as a founding father of modern conservatism.
3. **Constant, Benjamin (1767-1830).** Swiss-born, French liberal, a sustained critic of Rousseau and advocate of civil liberty and constitutionalism.
4. **Engels, Friedrich (1822-1895).** German socialist philosopher, collaborator and lifelong friend of Karl Marx. After Marx's death, Engel's writings had a profound effect upon the growing socialist movement and did much to popularise Marxism, but have subsequently been criticised for misrepresenting Marx's ideas.
5. **Friedman, Milton (b. 1912).** American economist, a leading exponent of monetarism and free market principles. Capitalism and Freedom (1962) and Free to Choose (1980) have had a powerful influence upon the New Right.
6. **Gandhi, Mohandas (1869-1948).** Indian spiritual and political leader, called Mahatma ('Great Soul'). Leader of Indian independence movement and

'exponent of non-violent non-cooperation' (Satyagraha).

7. **Godwin William (1756-1836).** British political philosopher and novelist, best known for 'An enquiry concerning political justice (1793), which advanced anarchist and utopian principles.

8. **Hegel (1770-1931).** German philosopher, whose complex writings inspired a generation of German intellectuals, the 'young Hegelians', including Marx and Striner. The philosophy of right (1821) influenced both liberal and fascist conceptions of the state.

9. **Hobbes, Thomas (1588-1679).** English philosopher and political theorist, best known for his social contract, defence of monarchical absolutism, developed in Leviathan (1651).

10. **Jefferson, Thomas (1743-1825).** American political philosopher and statesman, third president of the United States (1801-9). A leading advocate of natural rights and social contract theories, clearly reflected in the Declaration of Independence (1776).

11. **Kropotkin Peter (1842-1921).** Russian Anarchist. A Scientist and anarcho-communist was outlined in Manual Aid (1897) and whose vision of a decentralised society of the future was described in fields, factories and workshops (1901).

12. **Locke, John (1632-1704).** English philosopher and politician. A social contract theorist who placed special weight upon natural rights, his views had considerable impact upon early liberalism, especially his Two Treaties of Government (1690).

13. **Lovelock, James (b. 1919).** British scientist and environmentalist thinker, best known for his highly influential Gaia (1979).

14. **Marx, Karl (1818-1883).** German philosopher economist and political thinker. An active revolutionary and founder of the First International. His work provided the basis of much of nineteenth century socialist thought and greatly influenced communism in the twentieth century. His classic work was the three volume capital (1867, 1885 and 1894), his best known and most accessible work is the Communist Manifesto (1848).

15. **Mill, John Stuart (1806-1873).** English philosopher, economist and politician. A major exponent of liberalism, his most influential work includes On Liberty (1859), Considerations on Representative Government (1861), and the Subjection of Women (1869).

16. **Mitchell Juliet (b. 1940).** British socialist feminist and psycho-analyst. Her best known work is Women's Estate (1971). In Phychoanalysis and Feminism (1974) she showed a sympathy for Freudian analysis, unusual within feminism.

17. **Montesquieu (1689-1755).** French political philosopher, An admirer of British constitutionalism, who in his great work. The Spirit of Laws (1748) developed the doctrine of the separation of powers.

18. **Mosca, Gaetano (1857-1941).** Italian political sociologist best known as the founder of eliticism, most clearly developed in the Ruling Class (1896).

19. **Nietzsche, Friedrich (1844-1900).** German Philosopher and cultural critic. His complex and ambitious work, including. Thus Spake Zarathustra (1883-4), Beyond Good and Evil (1886) and on the Genealogy of Morals (1887), has influenced fascism, in part because his books were edited and his views misrepresented by his sister Elizabeth after his death.

20. **Nozick, Robert (b. 1938).** American political philosopher best known for Anarchy, State and Utopia (1974), which restated the classical liberal case for minimal state and rejected both economic management and social welfare.

21. **Oakeshott, Michael (1901-1991).** British political philosopher. An influential conservative theorist, his political ideas were most systematically developed in Rationalism in Politics and other Essays (1962) and on Human Conduct (1975).

22. **Owen, Robert (1771-1858).** British socialist, Established a model village in New Lanark, a communitarian project in America at Net Harmony and supported the emergent co-operative and trade union movements. His best known work, A New View of Society (1812-3) emphasised that personal character is wholly determined by environment.

23. **Pareto, Vilfredo (1848-1923).** Paris-born, Italian economist and political philosopher. A vigorous opponent of socialism and democracy and, with Mosca, the originator O. Elitism. His major work was The Mind and Society (1916).

24. **Proudhon, Pierre-Joseph (1809-1865).** French anarchist and founder of mutualism, best known for What is property? (1841).

25. **Rawts, John, (b. 1921).** American philosopher. A Theory of Justice (1971) did much to re-establish the status of political philosophy and has influenced both modern liberalism and social democracy.

26. **Rosseau, Jean Jaques (1712-1778).** French moral and political philosopher. An advocate of popular sovereignty and direct democracy, his ideas, particularly those developed in social contract (1762), have influenced liberalism, socialism, anarchism and, some argue, totalitarianism.

27. **Smith, Adam (1723-1790).** Scottish economist and philosopher. The founder of modern political economy, his The Wealth of Nations (1776) was the first systematic attempt to explain the workings of the economy in market terms.
28. **Sorel, Georges (1847-1922).** French philosopher and theorist of syndicalism. His major work Reflections on Violence (1908), proposed that socialism could be brought about by the 'myth of the general strike' a notion that subsequently influenced fascism.
29. **Spencer, Herbert (1820-1903).** British philosopher and sociologist. Best known as an exponent of social Darwinism, most clearly expressed in The Man Versus the State (1884).
30. **Tawney, Richard Henry (1880-1962).** British historian and social philosopher. An influential exponent of ethical socialism, developed in books like The Acquisitive Society (1921) and Equality (1931).
31. **Thoreau, David Henry (1817-1862).** American Author and radical. Walden (1854) has influenced environmentalism and the back to nature movement, while the more political 1849 essay 'Civil Disobedience' developed radical individualist principles.
32. **Tolstoy, Leo (1828-1910).** Russian novelist, best known for war and peace, advocate of moral purity.
33. **Tucker, Benjamin (1854-1939).** American anarchist and publisher. A leading exponent of individualist anarchism, developed between 1881 and 1908 in his magazine Liberty and in Instead of a Book (1893).

GLOSSARY OF TERMS AND CONCEPTS

This glossary provides brief definitions of key terms or concepts used in the text. These definitions are neither exact nor comprehensive but merely provides an indication of what these terms mean in political discourse.

achieved status. The condition of earning one's place in society through effort and ability. Contrast with *ascribed status.*

affirmative action. The attempt to promote equality of opportunity by providing assistance to members of groups, such as women and racial minorities, that have been the victims of discrimination.

alienation. Marx adapted this term from Hegel's philosophy to describe the separation or estrangement of persons or classes of people from their human potential. In capitalism, Marx claims, the worker's ability to control his or her labour is alienated.

anarchism. From the Greek *an archos,* meaning "no rule" or "no government," anarchism aims to abolish the state, replacing political relations with co-operative or voluntary ones.

anarcho-communism. The version of anarchism that aspires to a cooperative society in which all property is owned or controlled by the whole community.

anticolonial movements. Attempts by people in "Third World" countries to gain their independence from the rule of colonial (usually European) powers.

apartheid. The South Africa policy of "apartness," or separating the races, with whites holding political power.

aristocratic privilege. Rooted in the belief that one class of people is superior to others, this is the policy of reserving certain rights and opportunities—such as access to governing power—for the exclusive employment of the nobility.

arrogance of humanism. The Green charge that a "humanist" or anthropocentric outlook ignores or devalues the worth of other species of animals and plants and the environment that sustains them.

Aryans. Name given to a group of people from whom all Indo-European languages supposedly derive. Nazis believe that this people and their purest descendants are a "matter race" whose destiny is to conquer and rule—or exterminate—"inferior" races.

ascribed status. In contrast to *achieved status,* a society is based on *ascribed status* when a person is born into a particular social status—such as noble or serf—with little opportunity either to raise or lower his or her social standing.

atomistic conception of society. The view that society consists of individuals who are essentially unconnected to or independent of one other, like marbles on a tray. Contrast with the *organic conception of society.*

base (also **material-productive base**). Marx's metaphor for the "social relations" that constitute the "real basis" or foundation of material production—for example, the relationship of landowner to farmworker is part of the *base* of an agricultural society. See also *superstructure* and *materialist conception of history.*

bourgeoisie. Originally referred to those who lived in a market town (*bourg* in French), but later to the middle class—merchants and professional people—in general.

In Marx's terms, the *bourgeoisie* is the ruling class in capitalist society because it controls the *forces* (or *means*) *of production.*

capitalism. An economic system in which the major *means of production* are privately owned and operated for the profit of the owners of investors.

center. The moderate or "middle of the road" position in political terms as opposed to the more extreme positions of the *left* and *right.*

centralized control. Socialists who favour *centralized control* want to concentrate the control of all resources and decisions concerning production and distribution of goods in the central government.

class. A key concept in socialist, and particularly Marxian, analysis, *class* refers to one's socially determined location in the structure of social-economic relations. If you are part owner of the *forces* (or *means*) *of production,* you are a member of the *bourgeoisie or capitalist* class, if you are yourself a means of production, then you are a member of the working class, or *proletariat.*

classical (or traditional) conservative. Someone, like Edmund Burke, who believes that the first aim of political action must be to preserve the social fabric by pursuing a cautious policy of *reform.*

command economy. Favoured by the proponents of *centralized control,* this is the attempt to plan and direct economic production and distribution instead of relying on market forces.

communism. Originally used to describe any scheme of common or social control of resources, this term is now associated with Marxian socialism. For marx and the Marxists, the communal ownership and control of the *forces* (or *means*) *of production* represents the fulfillment of human history. The culmination of a long-term revolutionary sequence, communist society subscribes to the principle, "From each according to ability, to each according to need."

communitarian. In general terms, anyone who wants to bind people together into a strong, mutually supporting society. In particular, the term is now used to describe those who criticize liberalism for putting too much emphasis on the rights and interests of individuals while ignoring the needs of the community as a whole.

corporativism. Benito Mussolini instituted this policy in Italy in an attempt to bring owners, workers, and government together to promote economic production and harmony.

counter-Enlightenment. This term refers to a diverse group of thinkers in the early and mid-nineteenth century who rejected some of the leading ideas of the *Enlightenment* philosophers.

critical Western Marxism. The position taken by a number of twentieth-century scholars, principally European, who accept most of Marx's critique of capitalism as a repressive social and economic system, but who reject Marxism-Leninism and concentrate their efforts on analyzing capitalism as a form of cultural domination that prevents people from being truly free and creative beings.

cultural conservatism. Closely connected to *classical conservatism,* this brand of conservatism is particularly suspicious of commerce, industry, and "progress," which threaten, it says, our relationship with nature and our respect for cultural pursuits.

cunning of reason. Hegel's phrase for the process by which intentional actions produce unintended, but nonetheless "rational," consequences that promote the development of Spirit through history.

decentralized control. In contrast to *centralized control,* some socialists want to disperse power by placing control of resources and production in the hands of people at the lowest possible level, such as the town or workplace.

deep ecology. A "biocentric" or life-centered philosophical, ethical, and political perspective that places that welfare of human beings on a par with other species and the conditions that nurture and sustain them.

democratic centralism. Lenin's attempt to combine democracy with central control of the revolutionary *vanguard party.* The party should encourage debate and discussion within its ranks before decisions are made, Lenin said. Once the leadership reaches a decision, however, debate must stop and all members must obey.

dialectic. Different versions of this method of reasoning are found in Socrates, Plato, Hegel, and Marx, among others. Generally speaking, *dialectic* is the process whereby opposite views of forces come into conflict, which eventually leads to the overcoming or reconciliation of the opposition in a new and presumably higher form.

dialectical materialism (or sometimes **DiaMat).** The Soviet Marxist-Leninist view that traces all social, economic, and political phenomena to physical matter and its motions. The phrase, never used by Marx, became standard during Stalin's era.

dictatorship of the proletariat (also **revolutionary dictatorship of the proletariat).** The form of government that Marx expected to provide the transition from the revolutionary overthrow of the *bourgeoisie* to the eventual coming of communist society. This interim or transitional state will presumably *wither away.*

ecology. As a scientific discipline, *ecology* is the study of the connections, interdependencies and energy flows within and between species and ecosystems. In its more recent political sense, however, *ecology* refers to a perspective that values the protection and preservation of the natural environment.

ecotage. Short for "ecological sabotage," this is a form of direct action practiced by Earth First! and other militant environmentalist groups. Such sabotage ranges from "monkey-wrenching"—"decommissioning" bulldozers, cutting pcwers lines—to "spiking" old-growth trees to save them from loggers.

elitism. Elitists believe that there is a small number of people in any society who either should or necessarily will lead or rule the rest.

empire. A political union of several states or peoples governed by a single sovereign power of ruler.

empirical. A statement or proposition is *empirical* if it describes or explains how things are—for example, "It is hotter in Arizona than in Minnesota." Usually contrasted with *normative.*

Enlightenment. The influential philosophical movement of the eighteenth century, especially in France, that proclaimed the triumph of reason and science over custom and superstition.

essentially contested concept. A concept—such as art, religion, democracy—that generals controversy because it lacks a complete set of clear standards for determining when something falls under the concept. Indeed, this openness or indeterminacy seems to be the nature or essence of these concepts.

ethnic cleansing. A euphemism for the systematic murder or removal of members of one nationality or ethnic group by another. Used by militant Serbian nationalists in the early 1990s to justify the expulsion and murder of Muslims and members of other ethnic groups supposedly standing in the way of a united Serbian nation.

fabian socialism. The British brand of socialism emphasizing the peaceful, piecemeal, and gradual transition from a capitalist to a socialist society.

false consciousness. A Marxian phrase referring to the false or distorted beliefs of members of a subordinate class who fail to understand their true position in society. These false beliefs work to the advantage of the ruling class because they prevent the subordinate class from seeing the cause of its oppression.

feudalism. Specifically, the social and economic system of medieval Europe that centered on the relationship of the lord, who promised protection and the use of land in exchange for service, and the vassal. More generally, *feudalism* refers to any similar agricultural society in which a relatively small number of people control the land while most others work it as tenants or serfs. Often associated with *ascribed status.*

forces of production (also **material forces of production, means of production,** or simply **productive forces).** Marx's phrase for the material means or resources that labour transforms into useful goods or commodities. Examples, include trees that are transformed into lumber, ores that are transformed into metal, and the labour necessary to accomplish the transformation.

gay. Someone who favours exclusive sexual relations with persons of the same sex.

gender. A central concept within feminist thought. It refers to the social construction and meaning of the categories "masculine" and "feminine." That is, what makes something "masculine" or "feminine" is largely determined by social attitudes and beliefs.

glasnost. The Russian word for "openness," used by Mikhail Gorbachev in the 1980s to signal a policy of greater tolerance and freedom in the U.S.S.R.

green politics. The gradual warming of earth's atmosphere due to the buildup of carbon dioxide (CO_2) that results from the burning of fossil fuels (oils, gas, coal, and so on) and the destruction of forests.

harm principle. The principle, defended by John Stuart Mill and others that we should be allowed to do whatever we want unless our actins harm or threaten harm to others.

homophobia. The fear of homosexuals and/or their real or imagined influence.

ideologue. Someone who is strongly committed to a particular ideology and works to promote its triumph over rival ideologies.

immiseration of the proletariat. The Marxian prediction that the working class or *proletarial* would become progressively worse off under *capitalism.*

imperialism. According the Lenin, the policy whereby capitalist countries conquer, colonize, and exploit. Third World countries. It represents, in Lenin's view, the "highest" and last stage of capitalist domination of the world economy. Also a central concept for Mao Zedong and other Marxist-Leninists.

individualist conservative. Someone who believes that government should promote individual liberty by protecting against foreign threats, but otherwise leave people alone to do as they see fit. Such a view may be closer to *neoclassical liberalism* than to other forms of conservatism.

innovation. According to Edmund Burke, *innovation* is change for the sake of change or novelty. The desire to innovate, Burke says, leads people to neglect or reject their time-tested customs. Contrast with *reform.*

irrationalism. The belief, associated with thinkers like Freud and LeBon, that human beings are moved more by instincts, urges, or subconscious forces than by reason.

land ethic. A phrase coined by ecologist Aldo Leopold to refer to an attitude of reverence and respect for the land and the myriad life-forms it sustains.

left (or **left-wing**). In political terms, a "leftist" is one who believes a significant, perhaps even radical, change in a new direction will lead to great improvement in social and economic arrangements. In general, socialists are on the *left,* not the *right* on *center.*

levelling. The effort, criticized by many conservatives, to diminish or eliminate the gap between the wealthiest and poorest members of a society. Critics maintain that these efforts promote mediocrity and reduce everyone to the same miserable level.

liberal democracy. In contrast to *people's* and *social democracy, liberal democracy* emphasizes the importance of individual rights and liberty, including the right to own private property.

libertarianism. Generally, the desire to expand the realm of individual liberty. Specifically, another name for *neoclassical liberals,* who argue that the only legitimate power of government is to protect the persons and property of its citizens. Some libertarian *anarchists* believe that all governments are illegitimate and immoral.

Malthus's law. The assertion that human population tends to grow faster than the resources required to sustain it. Specifically, population grows geometrically and resources arithmetically.

market socialism. The attempt to combine some features of a competitive market economy with public control of resources. For example, the people who work in a factory may jointly own it, but they must compete for profits with other worker-owned factories.

mass society. According to some critics, the abolition of traditional social hierarchies has produced a dangerously unstable society in which the common people—and the politicians and advertisers who appeal to their tastes—bring everything and everyone down to their own level.

master-slave dialectic. Hegel's account of the confrontation between an all-powerful master and his presumably powerless slave. The conflict between the two reveals that the master is dependent upon his slave, and the slave, by winning his struggle for freedom and recognition, liberates both himself and the master. Marx and later "liberation" ideologists also employ this parable of emancipation.

material forces of production (also **forces of production, means of production, or simply productive forces).** Marx's phrase for the material means or resources that labour transforms into useful goods or commodities. Examples include trees that are transformed into lumber, ores that are transformed into metal, and the labour necessary to accomplish the transformation.

materialism. The philosophical doctrine that all reality—social, political, and intellectual—is ultimately reducible to combinations of physical matter. Different versions can be found in Hobbes, in Engels, and in twentieth-century *dialectical materialists.*

materialist conception (or interpretation) of history. The Marxian framework for interpreting or explaining social change. The central idea is that changes in the material-productive *base* bring about changes in the *social relations of production* and the ideological *superstructure.*

mercantilism. The economic policy of promoting a country's wealth at the expense of other' by establishing *monopolies* and regulating foreign trade to favour domestic industry.

mixed constitution (or government). The *republican* policy of combining or balancing rule by one, by the few, and by the many in a single government, with the aim of preventing the concentration of power in any person or social group.

monopoly. Exclusive control of a commodity or market by a single firm.

nationalism. The belief that people fall into distinct groups, or nations, on the basis of a common heritage or birth. Each nation is then supposed to form the natural basis for a separate political unit, or nation-state.

nation-state. A political unit that unites the members of a single nation, or people.

natural right. A right that everyone has simply by virtue of being a person. Such a right can neither be granted nor taken away by any person or political authority.

negative freedom. In contrast to *positive freedom,* this is the absence of restraint. You are free, in this view, if no else is preventing you from doing what you want to do.

neoclassical liberalism. The belief that government is a necessary evil that should do nothing but protect the persons and property of its citizens. See *libertarianism.*

neoconservatism. Beginning among disenchanted *welfare liberals* in the 1960s *neoconservatism* advocates less reliance on government, an anticommunist foreign policy, and an emphasis on the value of work, thrift, family, and self-restraint.

normative. A statement or proposition is *normative* if it prescribes how things should be or judges what is good or bad—for example, "lying is wrong". Usually contrasted with *empirical* and/or descriptive.

opiate of the masses (or people). Marx's phrase for religion, which he believed dulled the critical capacity of oppressed people by directing their attention and hopes away from this life.

organic conception of society. In contrast to the *atomistic conception,* this view holds that the members of a society are connected and interdependent, like the parts of the body, and society itself is more than merely the sum of its parts.

original sin. The belief in Christian theology that the first sin—Adam's defiance of God in the Garden of Eden—has somehow infected all humanity.

orthopraxis. Literally, correct practice or action. Liberation theologians urge the Catholic Church, and Christians in general, to "act correctly" by working for justice for the poor and an end to oppression.

people's democracy. Favoured by Marxist-Leninists, this is the view that democracy is government by the Communist Party in the interests of the working class.

perestroika. The Russian word for restructuring, used by Mikhail Gorbachev in the 1980s to refer in particular to the restructuring of the Soviet Union's economy.

Physiocrats. French economic theories of the eighteenth century who believed that land is the basis of wealth and unrestricted competition promotes prosperity.

political absolutism. Any form of government in which the ruler (or rulers) has nearly complete power, unrestrained by law or other governing bodies.

polity. In Aristotle's theory, this is generally the best form of government : rule by the many, who are neither wealthy nor poor, in the interests of the whole community.

positive freedom. In contrast to *negative freedom,* this is the belief that freedom is not simply the absence of restraint, but also the power or ability to act and to develop one's capacities.

prejudice. In Burke's theory, this is the "latent wisdom" that societies accumulate through long experience and that usually provides a useful guide to conduct and policy.

proletariat. Originally the lowest class in ancient Rome, this is Marx's word for wagelabourers, the industrial working class.

racism. The belief that one race (usually one's own) is innately superior to other races or ethnic groups.

reactionary. Someone who wants to return to an earlier form of society or government. More generally, an extreme conservative.

reform. A gradual and cautious change that corrects or repairs defects in society or government and, according to Edmund Burke, is safer and wiser than *innovation.*

relations of production (or **social relations of production**). Marx's phrase describing the social division of labour—for example, investors, managers, supervisors, labourers—required to transfrom the *material forces of production* into useful goods.

religious conformity. The policy of requiring everyone in a society to follow or acknowledge the same religious beliefs.

Religious Right. The movement by evangelical fundamentalists, such as the Christian Coalition in the United States, to restore "traditional family values."

Renaissance. The period of the "rebirth" (re-naissance) of classical learning in fifteenth-and sixteenth-century Europe.

republic. A form of government by the people that includes the rule of law, a *mixed constitution,* and the cultivation of an active and public-spirited citizenry.

revisionists. The name given to later Marxists who attempted to amend or revise Marxian theory in light of developments after Marx's death.

revolution. Originally used to describe an attempt to restore or revolve back to a previous condition, since the French Revolution this word has meant a sweeping or fundamental transformation of a society.

revolutionary dictatorship of the proletariat (also dictatorship of the proletariat). The form of government that Marx expected to provide the transition from the revolutionary overthrow of the *bourgeoisie* to the eventual coming of communist society. This interim or transitional state will presumably *wither away.*

right (or right-wing). In opposition to the *left* and *center,* the people who occupy the *right* end of the political spectrum typically oppose change and prefer an established social order with firmly rooted authority. Both conservatives and fascists are usually considered *right-wing.*

secularism. The tendency to turn away from religious considerations and to emphasize the value of earthly life as a good in itself.

separatist movements. The attempt by a group of people who see themselves as a distinct nation to break away from another country in order to form their own *nation-state.*

sexism. The belief that one sex is innately superior to the other.

social contract. How do some people acquire authority over others? Some theorists, such as Thomas Hobbes and John Locke, have answered that individuals in a *state of nature* have in some way entered into an agrement, or *social contract,* to form political societies and establish governments, thus creating political authority.

Social Darwinists. A group of *neoclassical liberals* of the later nineteenth and early twentieth centuries who adapted Darwin's theory of evolution to social and political life, concluding that the struggle for survival between individuals is a natural feature of human life and government should not intervene.

social democracy. In this view democracy requires a rough equality of power or influence for every citizen, which may require, in turn, the redistribution of wealth and/or the social control of resources and property. Contrast with *liberal* and *people's democracy.*

social ecologists. In contrast to *deep ecologists,* this view attaches special importance to human life, but also holds that humanity is dependent upon—and responsible for—the environment that sustains it and other species of life.

social relations of production (or **relations of production**). Marx's phrase describing the social division of labour (for example investors, managers, supervisors, labourers) required to transform the *material forces of production* into useful goods.

speciesism. The belief that the human species is innately superior to other animal species.

state of nature. In the theories of Thomas Hobbes, John Locke, and Robert Nozick, among others, this is the condition in which people live before they create society and government. Everyone is free and equal in this state, an no one has authority over anyone else.

stewardship. An orientation emphasizing human beings' responsibility for protecting, preserving, and sustaining the natural and social environment for the sake of future generations.

superstructure (also **ideological superstructure**). Marx's metaphor for the set of beliefs, ideas, and ideals that justifies or legitimizes the social arrangements that constitute the foundation or *base* of society. See also *materialist conception of history.*

theocracy. A form of government in which religious leaders, who see themselves as agents of God (or the gods), try to enforce divine commands by making them the law of the land.

Tory democracy. This policy, initiated by the British Conservative leader Benjamin Disraeli, supported voting rights and other benefits for the working class in order to forge an electoral alliance between the upper and the working class against the Liberal Party.

totalitarianism. The attempt to control every aspect of a country's life—military, press, schools, religion, economy, and so on—by a single, all-powerful party that systematically smothers all opposition.

traditional (or **classical) conservative.** Someone, like Edmund Burke, who believes that the first aim of political action must be to preserve the social fabric by pursuing a cautions policy of *reform*.

utilitarianism. The view that individuals and governments should always act to promote *utility* or, in Jeremy Bentham's terms, the greatest happiness of the greatest number.

utility. Anything that has value for anyone has *utility,* or usefulness, for that person.

utopia. A term coined by Thomas More from Greek words meaning either "good place" or "no place," *utopia* now refers to a perfect society from which greed, crime, and other social ill have been banished.

utopian socialism. A phrase Marx and Engels used to denote the moralistic and unrealistic schemes of earlier socialists.

vanguard party. Lenin's term for the Communist Party, which is to take a tutelary or "leading role" in the overthrow of capitalism and the transition to communism.

welfare (or **welfare-state) liberalism.** In contrast to *neoclassical liberalism,* this form of liberalism regards government as a tool to be used to promote individual freedom, welfare, and equality of opportunity.

withering away of the state. Marx's description of the process whereby the interim *dictatorship of the proletariat* loses its reason for being and gradually ceases to exist.

SELECT BIBLIOGRAPHY

1. Aristotile, The Politics (Chicago : University of Chicago Press, 1985).
2. Bakunin, M., 'Church and State' in the Anarchist Reader, ed., Woodcock, London : Fontana, 1977.
3. Bell, D., The End of Ideology, Glencoe, III : Free Press, 1960.
4. Bentham, J., Introduction to the Principles of Morals and Legislation, ed., J. Burns and H.L.A. Hort, London : Athlone Press, 1970.
5. Berlin, I., Four Essays on Liberty, (London : Oxford University Press), 1969.
6. Bernstein, E., Evolutionary Socialism, (New York : Schocken), 1962.
7. Bookchin, M., 'Anarchism and Ecology' in The Aarchist Reader, ed., G. Woodcock, London : Fontana, 1977.
8. Burke, E., On Government, Politics and Society, ed., B. W. Hill, London : Fontana, 1975.
9. Capra, F., The Turning Point, London : Fontana, 1982.
10. Cecil, H., Conservatism, London and New York : Home University Library, 1912.
11. Chamberlain, H.S., Foundations of the Nineteenth Century, New York : John Lane, 1913.
12. Constant, B., Political Writings, Cambridge University Press, 1988.
13. Crewe, I., Values : 'The Crusade that Failed' in The Thatcher Effect, ed., D. Kavanagh and A. Seldom Oxford : Oxford University Press, 1989.

14. Crosland, C.A.R., The Future of Socialism, London : Cape, 1956.
15. Dahl, R., Who Governs? Democracy and Power in an American City, New Haven : Yale University Press, 1961.
16. Darwin, C., On the Origin of Species, London : Dent, 1972, New York : New American Library, 1986.
17. Elshtain, J.B., Public Man, Private Woman, Oxford : Martin Robertson, 1981, Princeton : Princeton University Press, 1981.
18. Faure, S., 'Anarchy-Anarchist' in the Anarchist Reader, *ed.,* G. Woodcock, London : Fontana, 1977.
19. Firestone, S., The Dialectic of Sex, London : Women's Press, 1980.
20. Friedman, M., Capitalism and Freedom, Chicago : University of Chicago Press, 1962.
21. Gandhi M., Selected Writings of Mahatma Gandhi, ed., R., Duncan, London : Fontana, 1971.
22. Gilmour, I., Inside Right : A Study of Conservatism, London : Quartet Books, 1978.
23. Godwin, W., Enquiry Concerning Political Justice, ed., K.C. Carter, Oxford : Oxford University Press, 1971.
24. Goldsmith E., Blue Print for Survival, Harmondsworth : Penguin, 1972.
25. Goodman, P., 'Normal Politics and the Psychology of Power,' in The Anarchist Reader, ed., G. Wood Cock London : Fontana, 1977.
26. Gould, B., Socialism and Freedom, London : Macmillan, 1985, Wakefield, N.H. Longwood, 1986.
27. Green, T.H. Works, ed., R., Nettleship, London : Oxford University Press, 1988, New York : AMS Press, 1984.
28. Hegel, G.W.F., The Philosophy of Right, trans. T.M. Knox Oxford : Clarendon Press, 1942.
29. Hobbes, T., Leviathan, ed.
30. Jefferson, T., 'The United States Declaration of Independence', in Human Rights Reader, ed., W., Laqueur and B. Rubin, New York : Meridan, 1979.

31. Kropotkin, P., Mutual Aid, London : Henemann, 1902, Cheektowaga, N.Y. Black Rose Books, 1988.
32. Lindbloom C., Politics and Markets, New York : Basic Books, 1977.
33. Locke, J., Two Treaties of Government, Cambridge : Cambridge University Press, 1962, New York : New American Library, 1965.
34. Marx, K. and Engels, F., Selected Works, London : Lawrence and Wishart, 1968.
35. Michels, R., Political Parties, Glencoe : Fress Press, 1958.
36. Mill. J.S., On the Subjection of Women, London : Dent, 1970, Allington Heights, III : Harlan Davidson, 1980.
37. Millett, K., Sexual Politics, London : Virago, 1977, New York : Simon and Schuster, 1990.
38. MitChell, J., Women's Estate, Harmondsworth : Penguin, 1971.
39. Montesquell C. de., The Spirit of Laws, Glencoe III : Fress Press, 1969.
40. Mosca, G., The Ruling Class, Trans. and ed., A. Livingstone, New York : McGraw Hill, 1939, Des Plaines, III Greenwood, 1939.
41. Pareto V., The Mind and Society, London : Cape 1935, New York : AMS Press, 1935.
42. Plato, The Republic, Trans. H.D. Lee, Harmondsworth : Penguin, 1955, New York : Random, 1983.
43. Proudhon P.J., What is Property? Trans : B.R. Tucker, London : Dover Publications, 1971.
44. Rawls, J., A Theory of Justice, London : Oxford University Press, 1972.
45. Rothbart, M., For a New Lib^rty, New York : Macmillan, 1978.
46. Rousseau, J.J., The Social Contract and Discourse, ed., G.D.H. Cole, London : Dent, 1913, Glencoe, III : Free Press, 1969.
47. Smith, A., An Enquiry into the Nature and Causes of the Wealth of Nations, Chicago : University of Chicago Press, 1976.

48. Sorel, G., Reflections on violence, Trans., T.E. Hulme and J. Roth, New York : Macmillan, 1950.

49. Spencer, H., On Social Evolution : Selected Writings, Chicago : University of Chicago Press, 1967.

50. Tawney R.H., The Acquisitive Society, London : Bell, 1921, San Diego : Harcourt Brace Jovanovic, 1955.

51. Tawney, R.H., Equality, London : Allen and Unwin, 1969.

52. Thoreau, D.H.D., Walden and 'Civil Disobedience', Harmondsworth : Penguin, 1983.

53. Tocque Ville de., A., Democracy in America, London : Fontana 1968, New York : McGraw, 1981.

54. Wollstone Craft, M., A Vindication of the Rights of Women, ed., C.W. Hagelman, New York : Norton, 1967.

INDEX